HARDPRESS

ISBN: 9781407640730

Published by:
HardPress Publishing
8345 NW 66TH ST #2561
MIAMI FL 33166-2626

Email: info@hardpress.net
Web: http://www.hardpress.net

In Camp on the Big Sunflower

by

Lawrence J. Leslie

TABLE OF CONTENTS

CHAPTER I.

an alarm in the camp.

"hey, bandy-legs, what d'ye suppose ails toby there?"

"he sure looks like he'd just seen a ghost, for a fact, steve. where are max and his cousin owen just now?"

"oh, they walked down along the river bank to look for signs of fresh-water clams. so we'll just have to run things ourselves, bandy. hello! there, toby, what under the sun are you staring at?" and the boy called steve jumped to his feet as he called out.

it was night in the woods, with a cheery camp fire blazing close to where the restless river fretted and scolded along its crooked course.

the boy called toby, whose last name happened to be jucklin, also scrambled to his feet when thus hailed by his campmate, steve dowdy.

he was a broad-shouldered chap, unusually husky in build, and apparently as strong as an ox; but all his life poor toby had been afflicted with an unfortunate impediment in his speech that gave him no end of trouble.

when the third boy also stood erect it was plain to see how he came by his name. his legs were bowed, and appeared too short for his body. "now open up and tell us what you saw, toby," demanded steve, who was by nature inclined to be what his chums called "bossy."

"l-l-land's sake, didn't you s-s-see it, fellows?" asked the troubled one, his voice trembling with the excitement under which he was laboring.

"stick a pin in him, steve," advised bandy-legs; "that's the easiest way to make him talk straight english, you know."

"don't you dare try it, now, i tell you," warned the other, forgetting to even stutter in his indignation. "i'm going to tell you about it just when i'm good and ready. g-get that, now?"

"please commence then, toby," pleaded the shorter boy. "was it a real ghost you saw, or a snake? i'm terribly set against the crawlers, you remember."

"s-shucks! 'twan't no s-snake, bandy; i give you my word for that. but it had the awfulest glittering eyes you ever s-saw, boys."

"wow! listen to that for a starter, will you?" cried steve.

"keep going, toby; don't let up now," begged the boy with the crooked legs.

"i just couldn't make out for sure, b-but b-back of the eyes i thought i could see----"

"oh, what?" asked bandy-legs, feverishly.

"a long body just l-like that of a b-b-b----" toby seemed to swell up as he tried in vain to say the word he wanted, but it was apparently hopeless.

"why don't you whistle, toby, you silly?" cried steve.

"yes, that always helps you out, you know," the short boy declared, as he clapped a hand on the shoulder of the now red-faced stammerer.

upon which toby screwed up his rather comical face, puckered his lips, and emitted a sharp whistle.

strange to say, the action seemed to cure him for the time being of his trouble.

"was it a bear?" asked bandy-legs, impatiently.

"come off," remarked the other; "i was only going to say it looked like a big cat."

"he means a wildcat, steve!" exclaimed one of those who listened with all his nerves on edge.

"or, perhaps, it might have been a panther," remarked steve, a tinge of eagerness in his voice, for steve wanted to distinguish himself while on this camping trip by doing some wonderful exploit.

"and here we stand like a lot of gumps, when our guns are within reach. right now that terrible beast may be making ready to jump on us."

as the short-legged boy spoke he made a flying leap in the direction of the tent that had been erected.

both of his campmates were at his heels, and doubtless quite as anxious as himself.

there was a confused series of sounds following their disappearance. then they came crawling out again, each one gripping some sort of weapon.

"now, show me your blessed old tiger cat!" cried steve, handling a double-barreled shotgun valiantly.

"yes, who cares for a measly wildcat; let him step up and get what's coming to him!" declared bandy-legs, who was waving the camp hatchet ferociously.

"i'm b-b-badgered if i c-c-care what it is right now. this rifle belonging to max h-h-holds six bullets, fellows," spluttered toby.

"listen!" exclaimed steve, with more or less authority in his voice.

"oh, what did you think you heard, steve?" asked the wielder of the hatchet. "was it a whine, a cry just like a baby'd make? i've heard that's the way these panthers act just before they spring. be ready, both of you, to shoot him on the wing."

"rats! it was voices i heard," declared steve.

"then it must be max and owen coming back to camp from the river," bandy-legs asserted.

"just as like as not," steve admitted.

"but what if the savage beast drops down on the shoulders of our chums?" said the other in tones that were full of horror.

"c-c-come on, b-b-boys!" panted toby.

"where to?" demanded steve. "i'm comfortable just as i stand. what's eating you now, toby jucklin?"

"d-d-didn't you see, we've j-j-just got to warn our c-c-chums, and s-s-stand that t-t-terrible beast off? h-h-hurry, boys!"

"yes, i see _you_ hurrying," said steve, with a laugh; "why, you'd fall all over yourself, toby, and perhaps try to swallow our only hatchet in the bargain. besides, there's no need of our sallying forth to stand guard over max and owen, because here they come right now."

"sure they are," declared bandy-legs, "and mebbe we'll be able to find out whether it was a wildcat toby saw, a panther, or one of those awful injun devils they say come down here from the canada woods once in a long time."

"all right, you c'n laugh all you l-like," the boy who stammered said, obstinately; "but wait and s-s-see what max says."

the two boys, who strode into the camp just then, eyed the warlike group with positive surprise.

"what's going on here?" asked the one in the lead, who seemed to be a well-put-up lad, with a bold, resolute face, clear gray eyes, and of athletic build.

"why, you see, max," began steve in his usual impetuous way, "toby here thought he saw a hungry cat sizing us up, being in want of a dinner; and so we got ready to give him a warm reception."

"y-y-you b-b-bet we did!" exclaimed the party in question, shaking his hatchet ferociously.

the boy called max turned and looked toward his cousin owen, and there were signs of amusement in his manner.

"d'ye suppose it could have been a bobcat?"

steve went on, he having his own opinion, which was to the effect that toby had imagined things.

"suppose we find out?" suggested max, promptly.

"oh, no use asking *him*!" declared steve. "as soon as he tries to tell he gets to tumbling all over himself. he saw a pair of staring eyes, and imagined the rest. for my part, i've made up my mind 'twas only a little old owl."

bandy-legs laughed, while toby grunted his disgust.

"huh! think so, d-d-do you, mister know-it-all? j-j-just you wait and s-s-see," he remarked.

"wait for what?" demanded the scoffing steve.

"why, max is g-g-going to find out," asserted toby. "g-g-guess owls don't leave tracks, d-d-do they? well, max c-c-can soon tell us. huh! an owl!"

"oh, i reckon we'll soon be able to settle that part of it, all right," said max, soothingly, for he saw that his two friends were growing a little too earnest in their dispute.

"t-t-told you s-s-so," chuckled toby.

"now, first of all, toby, answer me a few questions, please," began max, steadily.

"s-s-sure i will; just c-c-crack away," the other piped up, cheerfully enough.

"sit down again in exactly the same place where you were at the time you saw these yellow eyes staring at you--they were yellow, all right, i suppose?" max continued.

"r-r-reckon i did s-s-say that," admitted toby, "b-b-but i might's well confess right n-n-now that i couldn't s-s-say for sure whether the eyes were g-g-green or y-y-yellow. all i k-k-know is they s-s-stared like anything at me."

"listen to him, would you!" exclaimed steve; "he's backing off his perch i tell you, taking water to beat the band."

"t-t-tain't so," stoutly declared toby. "i s-s-saw the eyes, and believed i c-c-could make out all the rest. g-g-go on, max; what's next?"

"are you sitting in the same place?" asked the other, quietly.

"i am," replied toby.

"now point exactly to the spot where, as you say, you saw the staring eyes," max went on.

"t-t-that's easy done. s-s-see where that bunch of wintergreen p-p-pokes up l-like the tuft of an injun's war bonnet--r-r-right there it was, max."

"all right," remarked the other, quickly. "now, the rest of you just hold your horses a bit and give me a chance to look around."

"you bet we will," declared bandy-legs.

"if anybody can find out the facts, max will," asserted steve.

the four boys watched with considerable interest to see what max would do. they had the greatest confidence in this chum, whose knowledge of things pertaining to the woods far exceeded that of any other member of the club.

first of all max stepped to the fire, and they could see that he was looking it over carefully.

"he's after a torch, that's what," asserted steve.

"s-s-sure he is," echoed toby.

"there, he's found what he wants," declared the boy with the crooked legs; "and it's a jim dandy one, too. now he's heading for the place you saw your big cat, toby."

"n-n-never said 'twas *my* cat!" flashed up the other, aggressively.

"well, you're the only one that saw the beast, anyhow," declared bandy-legs, stoutly.

"oh, let up on all that talk, fellows, and watch what max does," steve broke in, impatiently.

"and," remarked owen hastings, speaking for the first time, "if it should turn out to be any sort of a wild animal, look out how you shoot."

"i s-s-should s-s-say yes," added toby. "g-g-go mighty slow, boys, w-w-while our c-c-chum is in front."

"then don't you think of throwing that tomahawk, toby, remember," cautioned bandy-legs.

"shucks! you're only t-t-talking to hear yourself," grunted the other, in scorn.

meanwhile max had advanced, torch in hand.

he gave no evidence of any concern, and to all appearances seemed to take very little stock in the possibility of meeting with some species of dangerous wild beast.

they saw him bend down, and at the same time thrust the blazing fagot of wood closer to the ground.

"he's discovered something, sure as you live, and i bet you it's a track," asserted bandy-legs.

"huh! s-s-see him pickin' something up. p'r'aps it's an owl's feather," sneered toby.

"now he's beckoning to us to come on, fellows!" cried the eager steve.

with that the entire bunch started forward, filled with a desire to learn what max had discovered.

he was smiling as they hurriedly approached, and yet at the same time the frown upon his face told that max found himself puzzled.

"say, was it a w-w-wildcat?" bubbled forth toby.

"or a big virginia horned owl?" demanded steve.

max shook his head to both questions.

"nixy, fellows, you've got another guess coming," he remarked, soberly. "fact is, the eyes toby saw staring at him through the bushes belonged to a half-grown boy, and a badly scared one at that!"

CHAPTER II.

treasure hunting.

strange to say, toby, usually the last to gather his wits together, was on this occasion the first to give expression to his overwrought feelings.

"gee! that's a s-s-screamer you're g-g-giving us, max," he burst out with.

"but what makes you say it's a boy, max; why not a man, when you're about it?" asked the skeptical steve.

max held up something he clutched in his hand.

"that's a boy's cap, reckon you'll all admit," he asserted, quietly.

"it sure looks like it," admitted bandy-legs, bending forward to examine the article in question.

"and a mighty tattered cap in the bargain, i should say," remarked owen, who was something of a bookworm, filled with a theoretical knowledge concerning subjects that, as a rule, his cousin max had personal acquaintance with.

"all right," max went on, "i found this here, right where toby saw the staring eyes. but that isn't all, fellows. look down where i point, and tell me what you see."

bandy-legs and toby could not make anything out of the queer-looking marks they saw revealed by the light of the torch.

with the others it was different.

"somebody's been kneeling here, for a fact," declared steve.

"here's where his knees pressed in the earth; and you can see how his toes dug holes yonder," owen remarked, pointing.

"just so," max went on; "and when you notice how short the distance between knees and toes is, you'll agree with me it was a boy."

"that's all right, max," spoke up steve; "but why would he be a scared boy--why didn't the chump walk right into camp and join us?"

"perhaps this boy has some reason to be afraid. perhaps he got an idea in his head that we'd come up here to hunt for him! and when he saw toby looking straight at him, he fell into a regular panic right away."

"you m-mean he s-s-s-s----" and finding that the word was going to prove too much for him toby quickly puckered up his lips, gave a little whistle, and wound up by speaking the objectionable word as plainly as anyone could have done--"skedaddled?"

"yes, ran away as fast as he could," max continued. "i'm sure of that from the tracks he made, and only wonder how he could have done the same without you hearing him."

"where are his tracks?" asked steve.

"yes, show 'em to us, max," added bandy-legs.

"look here, and here, and here, then. you can see by the size that these footprints were made by a boy. and, yes, his shoes are just about falling to pieces in the bargain. he's got one tied with a piece of twine, wrapped several times around."

"gosh! however do you know that, max?" asked the astonished bandy-legs.

"why, once you learn how to read signs, it's as easy as falling off a log," laughed max, as he proceeded to show them just how he figured things out.

"that's t-t-too bad," muttered toby.

"just why?" inquired max.

"if he'd only had the n-n-nerve to step up, and m-m-make our acquaintance, there's that bully pair of m-m-moccasins, you know, i'd like to have g-g-given him. always pinch my t-t-toes dreadful. just f-f-fit him, i bet," declared toby, who had a very warm heart.

"well, it's too late now, because the fellow's far enough away by now," commented max.

"perhaps we might happen to run across him some other time?" suggested steve, consolingly.

"like as not," the other remarked, "and now, let's return to the camp, and think of what we'll have for supper. i'm as hungry as a bear, for one."

"same here," declared bandy-legs enthusiastically; for, though short of stature, he was known to have full stowage capacity when it came to disposing of appetizing food.

there was soon more or less of a bustle around the camp. each one seemed willing to help, and from the orderly way in which they went about their several tasks it was evident that these campers had reduced things to something of a system.

and while the supper is in process of preparation it might be as well for us to learn a little more about these five lively lads.

they belonged in the town of carson, which lay some fifteen miles to the south of the camp.

always warm friends and chums, they had lately organized themselves into a little club, which they called the outing boys of carson. the main object of this association was camping out, and having a good time generally. but max and owen had by degrees conceived ideas far in advance of these early plans.

it was on account of these ambitious projects that they had now come up into this wilderness where the boys of carson were never known to penetrate before.

max had a good home, and his cousin owen, who was an orphan, lived with him.

steve was the only son of the leading grocer in carson, which fact more than once aroused the keen jealousy of toby jucklin, who, like bandy-legs, never seemed able to get enough to eat.

toby himself lived with an uncle, and perhaps this gentleman did not fully appreciate the enormous appetite of a growing boy, and failed to satisfy his needs. besides, nathan jucklin was known all over that section as close-fisted, and capable of "squeezing a penny."

then there was bandy-legs. of course he had a name by which he was known among his teachers at school and at home. it was clarence; but to every boy in town he went by the significant name of bandy-legs.

they had come up the narrow and tortuous evergreen river in a couple of old boats, capable of carrying all the camp material; though so leaky that frequent baling out was necessary in order to keep things dry.

sometimes they had been able to use the oars to advantage, and cover a mile or two in pretty good fashion.

then, again, they were compelled to use poles in order to push the boats; or, else going ashore, drag them by means of long ropes, for the rapids were swift.

it had taken them from early morning to nearly dusk to cover these fifteen-odd miles; but now that the camp was established, the tent up, the fire crackling, and supper being prepared, they forgot their tired backs and muscles.

"hey, max!" called out bandy-legs, turning around from where he was attending to the bubbling coffee.

"what is it?" asked the other, who had managed to arrange a temporary rude table, a slab of wood having been brought along for the purpose. "you forgot to tell us about it, don't you know?" the other went on. "somehow, all the excitement about that silly kid in the bushes knocked it clean out of my head."

"it did now, f-f-for a fact," spoke up toby. "so t-t-tell us what the p-p-p-p"-- whistle--"prospects are, won't you?"

max and his cousin exchanged a quick look, after which the former placed a finger on his lips.

"wait a little, toby," he said, cautiously. "when we gather around the festive board, and get our heads close together, i've got some bully good news to tell the bunch of you."

"h-h-hear that, will you, boys?" remarked toby, in more or less excitement.

"say no more now, please. how about that coffee?" max continued.

"s-s-she's cooked to a turn, and i h-h-hope the rest of the g-g-grub is ready, too."

"all right here," announced bandy-legs, seizing the frying pan, which was filled with potatoes, seasoned with a few onions, and hurrying over to where the low table had been arranged.

inside of five minutes they were busily engaged disposing of the savory mess.

five hungry lads can make away with considerable food, given the chance; but all due allowance had been made for even the astonishing appetites of toby and bandy-legs, when making preparations for the feast.

once the edge was taken off their appetites, and the boys remembered the promise made by max.

"now tell us what luck you had, max," steve asked, as he broke open a fresh paper package of crackers, and appropriated a generous portion of cheese.

"y-y-yes, that's the t-t-ticket!" exclaimed toby.

"i did promise, didn't i?" max started out to say; "and it's time i kept my word. you know the idea wasn't mine at all, but came from owen here, who had been reading up on the subject. we wanted to discover some way of earning a nice little sum of money this summer, in order to carry out certain plans we've got in our minds; and among all the schemes hatched up, his one struck us as the smartest."

"besides, it gave us just the jolliest chance to come up here and pitch camp," asserted steve.

"something we'd been talking of doing for ever so long, fellows," bandy-legs put in.

"all of which is true," max went on to say. "well, what was this bright little idea owen sprung on us! nothing more nor less than a treasure- hunting expedition. only, instead of trying to unearth the gold and jewels some captain kidd of these northern woods has hidden away, we expect to find something in the way of gems that no mortal eye has ever looked on up to now."

apparently these words of max gave the others quite a thrill, for they exchanged looks, and their faces betrayed evidence of intense interest.

"owen had taken a great deal of stock in this new industry of finding pearls in mussels, or fresh-water clams," max went on. "he managed to learn that long ago our river had been pretty well stocked with these shellfish, though the town people had eaten them up clean. but owen believed, and i agreed with him, that some miles up-stream the chances were we might find a good lot of mussels, big fellows that had never been disturbed except by some hungry 'coon or fox."

"and so we just made up our minds to start out on what seemed to be an innocent camping trip," broke in steve, chuckling. "that would give us all the chance we wanted to see whether there was anything in this pearl- fishing business along fresh-water streams."

"and we're here, all right, ready for work," remarked bandy-legs. "would you mind passing me that frying pan, owen? it's a shame to waste such a lot of tasty grub."

"huh! n-n-no danger," grunted toby, enviously.

"we had to hurry for all we were worth to get up here before dark," steve remarked; "for owen said the best place would be at the junction of the two little streams that go to make the evergreen. and so we didn't have any chance to make a hunt on the way up."

"but we saw lots of empty shells, you know," broke in bandy-legs.

"yes, looked as if muskrats, or something like that, had been living off mussels right along," steve admitted.

"and so, while we made camp, our two learned leaders strolled up the river known as the big sunflower to see what the chances were for a crop," bandy-legs went on.

"now, please make your report, max, because, you see, we're just burning up with anxiety to know. a whole lot depends on whether we've come up here on a fool's errand or not. did you find what you expected? are the full shells here a-plenty?"

and, smiling at the eagerness of steve, max drew out several large mussels from his pockets, which he clapped upon the rude table.

"they're here, all right, boys," he said, earnestly, "but as to whether we'll find any pearls in the same, that remains to be proven."

CHAPTER III.

what owen knew.

"well, i declare, is that the kind of mussel they've been finding pearls in?" demanded steve dowdy, as he took one of the long-shaped bivalves in his eager hands, the better to examine it.

"they agree with the description to a dot," owen replied, confidently; "and, to my mind, these seem particularly fat and promising."

"t-t-tell me about that, now, will you?" gasped toby, who was also examining a prize. "s-s-say, max, why looky here, i've picked up these s-sort of c-c-clams many a t-time when d-diving."

"i reckon we all have, and opened them, too, to eat," replied max, with a good-natured laugh; "but not being wise to the pearl racket at the time, it never struck us that we ought to examine the shellfish closely before swallowing."

"bet you more'n one pearl has gone down my red lane then," grinned bandy-legs; "because, you see, i always used to be mighty fond of fresh or pickled mussels. say, perhaps i'm a walking jewelry shop right now, fellers. mebbe i'm carrying around a whole pearl outfit. wow! it makes me feel uneasy-like."

"d-d-don't you worry any, my b-b-boy," broke in toby; "no danger of anybody t-t-trying to k-k-kidnap you, even if your pouch was lined with p-p-pearls."

"that's wise of you to say such kind things, toby! i'll remember it, too," said the other, reproachfully.

"but, see here," remarked steve, "what's to hinder us from breaking open these mussels right now, and finding out if they've got anything worth saving sewed up inside?"

"be sure and keep the meat, then, fellows," broke out the boy with the crooked legs. "two apiece all around means ten, and that ought to make a nice little dish of stewed mussels."

"yes, j-j-just so, for t-two," asserted toby.

each boy thereupon set eagerly to work opening the pair of shellfish that had fallen to his share. being unfamiliar with the methods employed they were doubtless all more or less clumsy. one by one they succeeded in accomplishing the task, and immediately set to work examining the contents for any sign of a prize.

silence reigned for several minutes. then max addressed his four chums, inquiring:

"are you all through?"

an affirmative answer came from each one of the others in turn.

"what luck, owen?" asked the master of ceremonies, turning upon his cousin.

"nothing doing here," came the response.

"how about you, bandy-legs?" max went on.

"all a bluff; nary a show of color," was the way the disappointed one made answer.

"steve?"

"nixy, nothing from me. i've searched every particle of the blooming old things, but pearls seem to be as scarce as hens' teeth. perhaps these ain't the right kind of fresh-water clams, after all."

"yes, they are," replied max; "and how is it with you, toby?" and there seemed to be something like confidence in the way he turned to the last member of the ranger boys' club, for he had not been secretly watching toby for nothing.

"i found only a r-r-rotten little p-p-pebble," replied toby.

"let me see it, then?" asked max.

"oh! c-c-come now, max, you're j-just trying to string me. s-sure that ugly little crooked thing could never be a valuable pearl?" remonstrated toby.

"perhaps not, toby, but all the same i'd like to take a look at it," answered max.

"fork over, toby," commanded bandy-legs, with almost too great a vein of authority in his voice.

15

the stutterer looked halfway belligerent; then, as if thinking better of his first desire for a wordy conflict, he passed the tiny object across the table to max.

both he and owen examined it by the aid of a strong magnifying glass.

"it's a pearl, all right," announced max, finally.

"oh! joy! joy!" exclaimed toby, ready to leap to his feet and begin a jig.

"but without any particular commercial value," owen said, once again freezing the enthusiasm of the stammering, excited toby.

"all the same, it ought to encourage us to begin work dredging the big sunflower," remarked steve, as he started in to examine the first find of the expedition.

"it certainly will," owen declared. "but, see here, max, what are you grinning about?"

"he's found something in his old oyster, bet you a cooky!" ejaculated bandy-legs, excitedly.

"is that so, max? did you see our friend toby, here, and go him one better?" asked steve.

max was still smiling broadly.

"you've got me up against the fence, fellows," he admitted. "caught me with the goods on, as they say. yes, it's a fact, i *did* find something in that second tough old mussel shell i opened."

"was it really a decent pearl, max?" pleaded steve.

"look for yourselves, boys, and tell me what you think."

as he spoke, max opened his left hand.

the action allowed a small, milk-white object, much smaller than a pea, to escape. it rolled upon the board which composed the table; and as the fire burned brightly, all of the boys could easily examine it.

one by one they picked the tiny white object up and held it at several angles, to see how the glow of the fire seemed to reflect in faint prismatic colors from its surface.

"say, this *is* a pearl, all right, and a jim-dandy one, too," declared steve, after he had had his turn at handling the discovery, "i ought to know, because my mother's got a string of the same--left to her by an old aunt over in england."

"owen, what d'ye suppose it's worth!" demanded max, turning on his cousin.

"well, now, you've got me there, fellows," declared the bookworm. "you see everything depends on how pure and perfect it happens to be."

"that's a fact," said steve, thoughtfully, as he feasted his eyes on the little beauty. "d'ye know, fellows, i've always been fond of pearls. why, when i was only a little kid my mother says i used to notice a ring my aunt wore, and would hang around her all the time, wanting to touch the pretty little gem. i reckon the old admiration still holds good."

steve even sighed as he reluctantly passed the new-found pearl along. max smiled to notice how his eyes seemed to follow it.

"well, we've proved one thing, sure," remarked bandy-legs, as he scraped the skillet carefully for the third time, evidently believing it was a sin to waste a single scrap of good food.

"yes," spoke up toby, who was watching this action with signs of disapproval, for he believed he would be compelled to complete his meal with crackers and cheese; "we k-k-know now there are p-pearls in some of these b-b-blessed old m-m-m"--whistle--"mussels, there!"

"but don't let's get too big notions, fellows," owen thought fit to put in just then.

owen was what his teacher at school always described as "conservative." he lacked the impulsive sanguine disposition of steve. at the same time he was no "croaker," and far from being a "doubting thomas."

owen often acted as a safety brake in connection with his chums. when some of them showed signs of rushing pellmell along the road, regardless of difficulties and unseen pitfalls, it was owen who would gently draw them in, and counsel caution.

they looked to him as a mentor, nor were any of them in the least offended when he restrained their headlong rush.

"in what way, owen?" asked steve.

"you see, it's like this," the other went on. "from what max and i learned, we don't fancy there can be any great quantity of these mussels up here. perhaps we won't find a single one along the other little stream, which they call the elder river."

"how about that, max?" asked bandy-legs.

"it's the simple truth. i was told we might get a few of the shellfish up along the big sunflower, but none in the water of the other creek," replied the one addressed.

"h-h-how do they account f-for that?" asked toby, always eager to learn.

"must be something in the water that prevents mussels from breeding in the elder," owen replied; and so great was the confidence those fellows placed in the knowledge of their bookworm chum that not one of them dreamed of disputing his theory.

"go on, please," steve remarked. "you had it on your tongue to say something more, didn't you, owen?"

"only this. we might scrape in a hundred, five hundred or a thousand shellfish, and not be able to duplicate this lovely little gem once."

"t-t-that's so," observed toby. "they s-s-say pearl hunting's the b-b-biggest lottery in the whole w-w-world."

steve was sitting there with his elbows on the table, both hands holding his head, and his eyes glued on the pearl that lay between them.

"that would be a tough deal," he muttered. "i'd give a heap to have a handful of those pretty little things. my! just to think what luck to strike one the first pop."

"besides," owen went on, lowering his voice, as he seemed to cast a quick suspicious glance to the right and to the left, "that isn't all, fellows."

his manner somehow thrilled toby and bandy-legs. even steve raised his head to stare at owen, though it required an effort for him to break the strange spell the milk-white pearl seemed to have cast about him.

"tell us what you mean, owen," begged the broad-shouldered young samson, with the bowed legs.

"yes, p-p-please do, b-because you s-s-see, we're all worked up now."

"then listen, fellows," said owen, impressively. "it's only fair, as max and myself have decided, that you should know all we've found out."

"that's right," muttered steve. "as well as what we suspect," owen continued, in the same mysterious way.

steve was so deeply impressed with the seriousness of owen's manner, that, perhaps unconsciously, he allowed his hand to steal over to where the double-barreled shotgun leaned against the trees, and rest confidingly upon the same.

max had occasion to remember afterwards just how much steve was worked up.

"well, what was it?" asked bandy-legs, after owen had allowed some seconds to elapse.

"for the last half mile, when we were pushing up toward the forks of the river," owen went on, "we noticed that the empty shells along under the banks seemed to grow more numerous."

"yes, and all of us felt tickled to see it," broke in steve, "because it was a good sign. it told us the mussels were here, all right."

"and it also told us," owen continued, "that there were a lot of little fur-bearing animals living along the stream, with a mighty strong taste for fresh-water clams."

"as what?" asked bandy-legs.

"oh! mink, otter, muskrats, raccoons, and perhaps fisher. all these used to be plentiful through these parts in years gone by. i've heard of men trapping them, but of late it's been lost sight of, so i reckon they've increased at a great rate."

"well, i don't see anything about that to bother us much," argued steve. "i reckon there'll be plenty for all of us. what the minks and musquash get won't keep us from making our try, will it?"

"no," said owen. "but it wasn't that i was speaking about. the fact is, we made a disagreeable discovery a little while ago, when we went out to investigate--ran across a heap of mussel shells piled up by human agency, and not through that of fur-bearing animals in search of a meal."

the three others who heard this startling fact for the first time stared at owen, as if hardly able to grasp the full dimensions of the calamity that threatened their pet project.

CHAPTER IV.

the unknown shell gatherers.

steve was, as usual, the first to recover from the sudden shock.

"whew! that sounds like a tough deal, fellows!" he remarked, with a grimace. "here we are, thinking we've got the field all to ourselves; and expecting to spring a big surprise on the sleepy folks of carson when we come marching home with a pocketful of valuable fresh-water pearls, that would give the ranger boys all the money they need to carry out their pet plans. and squash! almost as quick as you can wink, it's all knocked into a cocked hat. yes, a tough deal, boys, and perhaps no more of these little beauties for us."

he picked up the lone pearl again, as if unable to wholly resist its attractions.

"huh! and instead of having the field all to ourselves, it looks like we might be poaching on the preserves of some other fellow."

bandy-legs gave voice to his bitter disappointment after this fashion.

"t-t-too bad," muttered toby, who seemed to feel that upon an occasion like this every member of the club ought to allow himself to be heard.

"say," broke out steve, suddenly, "perhaps it's that little prowler toby sighted spying on the camp?"

"i wonder!" exclaimed bandy-legs, his face lighting up with new interest.

"perhaps the boy may have some connection with the gathering of the shells," owen went on, "but it was a man's big footprint we saw alongside the pile of empties when we struck a match."

"what do you think about it, max?" suddenly asked steve, turning around to stare at the one he addressed.

max had apparently seemed quite content to let his cousin do the talking, for he had remained quiet during this discussion.

upon being directly appealed to, however, he was not at all backward about replying.

"i've been doing a heap of thinking since owen and myself examined that pile of shells," he started in to say, "and if you care to hear the conclusion i've come to, all right."

"you b-b-better b-b-believe we do, max," was toby's immediate explosion.

"don't hold back a thing," observed steve; "because we're all dyed-in-the- wool chums; and what concerns one concerns all."

"cough it up, max. we're holding our breath, you understand, wanting to know. and none of us come from missouri, either," bandy-legs observed, eagerly.

max smiled at the expressive way his comrades had of urging him on. nor could he fail to be deeply touched by their confidence in his ability to fathom the puzzle.

"i took occasion to examine some of those empty shells by the light of other matches," he continued; "and on many of them i was surprised to find plain marks of small teeth!"

"wow! i'm g-g-getting on to what you're going to spring on us!" exclaimed toby, whose wits were not slow, if his speech had that affliction.

"i don't believe any of those mussels had been opened by human hands," max went on to boldly declare. "whoever is up here must be collecting them just for the sake of the mother of pearl. you know, i suppose, that these shells are used for making pearl buttons and such things?"

"yes, they are worth so much a hundred pounds," remarked owen. "the price is high enough to pay some men for collecting them when they can be found in any decent quantities."

"then, max, you don't think these parties are onto the pearl racket--is that it?" asked steve.

"honest injun, boys, that's the conclusion i've reached after studying it out. they are just collecting the empty shells, and never dreaming how one little pearl like this would be worth perhaps a full ton of shells." and max took the prize from steve, who seemed a bit reluctant to let it go.

max had apparently made up his mind as to what would be a safe hiding place for the little beauty.

all of them watched him wrap the pearl in a wad of pink cotton, deposit this in a small cardboard box about two inches long by one wide, and half as thick; which, in turn, was carefully thrust into a haversack hanging from the center pole of the tent.

that same haversack was used as a "ditty" bag. all sorts of small articles, likely to prove useful in camp, were deposited in its capacious depths. and when anything was wanted, the boys usually searched in this leather pocket before proceeding to any trouble.

"a snug nest for our first prize, eh?" bandy-legs took occasion to remark, as he watched how carefully max pushed the little packet down into the depths of this depository.

"it sure ought to be safe there," steve declared, with a sigh as of genuine relief.

"nothing could happen to it, with five fellows sleeping around. and max is so ready to wake up that he'd even hear a cat moving," owen remarked, with a laugh.

"do you expect we'll have any trouble with these pearl-shell gatherers, max?" steve demanded.

"i hope not," was the ready reply. "we don't expect to interfere with their business at all. fact is, we'd just as lief turn over what shells we gather to these parties to pay for trespassing on their preserves."

"but not the pearls we find--if so be we're lucky enough to run across more?" flashed steve.

"surely not," max answered, sturdily. "they don't own this country; and i'm sure they've got no lease on the waters of the big sunflower. so we have just as much right up here as they do. but we're a peaceable crowd, you know; that's one of the leading rules in the constitution of the ranger boys' club."

"yes," chuckled bandy-legs, "we're set on having peace even if we have to fight for it."

"well," put in toby, aggressively, "all i c-c-can s-s-say is, they'd b-b-better think twice before t-t-trying to bother our crowd. we're only b-boys, but we've got rights."

"hear! hear!" broke out bandy-legs, clapping his hands as if to encourage the speaker.

"and we know how to s-s-stand up f-for 'em," wound up toby, shutting his teeth hard on the last word, and looking very determined.

"you bet we will," remarked steve. "i'd just like to see anybody have the nerve to try and steal that bully little gem we've captured first pop. my stars! don't i hope we'll have the mate to it in short order."

presently the talk drifted to other things connected with their home life in carson. the names of several boys were mentioned; and from the way bandy-legs and toby expressed opinions of those same school fellows, it appeared that they suspected the others of having watched their movements of late.

"lucky we played that fine trick," the former declared, "and started on our up-river voyage before daybreak, while ted shafter, amiel toots, shack beggs, and the rest of the gang were tucked away in their little trundle beds fast asleep."

"s-s-say, don't you b-b-believe there was a high j-j-jinks of a time to-day when ted f-f-found we'd slipped away, and nobody knew where?"

"but they know we had boats," remarked max, "because we caught one of the crowd spying on us. that's why we had to keep our stuff under lock and key, with old stump griggs to watch it."

"yes," complained steve, bitterly, "because a fellow as mean as ted is wouldn't stop a minute if he found a chance to upset our plans. ten to one the prowler old stump scared away night before last was ted himself; and i wouldn't put it past that bad egg to burn the boathouse down, just to get even with our crowd."

"but the outing boys don't scare worth a cent," declared bandy-legs, given to boasting a little more than any of his chums.

"oh, well!" observed max, cheerfully, "we expect to hide our boats in the morning, you know, and perhaps, even if ted and his scrappers do work up along this way, they won't find us. if we're wading in the river searching for mussels we're apt to hear them coming in time to get away."

"guess you're right there, max," said owen.

"sure thing," remarked bandy-legs. "there ain't a time but what some of tad's crowd are snapping at each other to beat the band. every little while a fight is on the carpet. takes tad half the time keeping peace in the family."

"huh!" chuckled steve. "i've seen him do it by knocking down both of the scrappers, just as neat as you please. ted likes that way of keeping the peace. it gives him exercise, you see, and makes the fellow respect him more 'n more."

the supper tins were washed, and for quite a long time the five boys sat around the crackling fire, talking, writing in their note books, and amusing themselves in many ways.

it was no longer dark.

a moon, slightly past the full, had crept above the horizon before they finished supper; and while the trees prevented those in camp from getting all the benefit of this fine sky lantern, for the most part the shadows that lurked in the woods were banished.

finally some of the boys began to show signs of sleepiness. toby was yawning about every minute, while bandy-legs rubbed his eyes and stretched himself, like a tired boy nearly always does.

"guess it's about time we turned in, fellows," max declared, himself feeling the effect of getting up at three o'clock in the morning in order to leave town before peep of dawn.

"that's what i say," agreed bandy-legs. "i'm sore all over from poling that clumsy old boat up-river. and once i hit the straw you'll never hear a peep from me till morning."

"move we adjourn!" sang out toby, so suddenly that he actually neglected to stammer.

"all in favor say 'aye'!" max proceeded to observe; and immediately a chorus of approval was the signal to send them hurrying into the tent.

ten minutes later and silence rested all over the camp on the big sunflower. a hungry raccoon came prowling around, eager to pick up what crumbs had fallen from their table. the big moon climbed higher and higher in the clear sky, and, mounting above the tops of the trees to the east, looked down, and smiled upon the peaceful scene.

max was a light sleeper, just as one of his comrades had declared.

no matter how sound his slumber appeared to be, if there happened to be any unusual movement in the camp it was sure to arouse him.

he did not know just how long he had been dead to the world at the time something moving caused him to open his eyes.

the moon had climbed so high that he knew some hours must have passed.

yes, there was certainly some one moving about in the tent. max, of course, first of all thought of ted shafter and his cronies, and wondered if, after all, the rival carson crowd could have found them out.

next his thoughts flew to the unknown shell gatherers, and a suspicion that perhaps one of them had invaded the camp, bent on stealing the valuable pearl, filled his mind.

this caused max to raise his head, and turn his eyes toward the tent pole where the haversack containing the precious pearl hung.

sure enough, there *was* some one standing there, and actually fumbling with the bag.

to the intense surprise of max he recognized the dimly seen figure.

it was steve.

CHAPTER V.

a puzzler for max.

max could hardly believe his eyes.

it seemed so remarkable for steve to be examining the haversack at this midnight hour.

perhaps the other had been dreaming, and as the pearl was much in his mind he may have gotten up to ascertain whether the little package still reposed safely in the pouch?

max came to this conclusion as he lay there and watched.

steve seemed to give a satisfied grunt presently. then he turned away, stepped gingerly over the forms of bandy-legs and toby, bent down for a few seconds, as if fumbling with his clothes, and still muttering to himself, finally crawled under his own blanket.

max was chuckling as he dropped back on his rude pillow made of leaves that had been crammed into a flour sack.

"guess steve is deeper in this pearl business than the rest of us," he muttered, "since he has to climb out of a warm blanket just to make sure nobody's got away with our first prize. well, he's welcome to stand guard. me to get some more sleep."

so little impression did the circumstance make upon max's mind that in less than five minutes he had drifted away once more to the borders of slumberland.

in the morning it was owen who awakened the balance of the campers.

"here, suppose you fellows show a leg, and take a dip in the creek," he announced, poking his head into the tent.

"i smell bacon!" cried bandy-legs, as he sat up hurriedly.

"and that must sure be the odor of c-c-coffee that comes s-s-stealing in here!" declared toby, bounding erect.

soon the four were floundering about in the cool waters of the big sunflower.

they did not prolong their bath because owen had declared breakfast almost ready. as bandy-legs remarked, they could take a dip at any old time; but breakfasts only cropped up once in every twenty-four hours.

and, hence, it was not long before they were seated around the table, enjoying the bacon and fried eggs, hominy and coffee, that the cook of the morning had provided; flanked by an abundance of home-made bread and country butter.

the conversation turned from one subject to another. first it was the chance of their being discovered and annoyed by the crowd that ran with ted shafter. then came talk of the mysterious shell gatherers, whose secret industry the sudden coming of the ranger boys might interfere with.

max was several times tempted to bring up the subject of the pearl, just to find an opportunity for asking steve if it had been a bad dream that sent him from his warm blanket to make sure the little packet was safe.

then he decided to hold back just a little longer, and let one of the others start the ball rolling.

no doubt steve would volunteer a satisfactory explanation without being prodded, given time.

sure enough, it was bandy-legs who brought the conversation around to the subject of the pearl.

he and toby seemed to disagree as to the size of the prize, the latter stubbornly insisting that it was as large as a little marble.

"aw! rats! what is getting you, toby!" exclaimed bandy-legs, in disgust. "sure you must have been dreaming over it, and things have been growing all night. i tell you it was smaller'n a pea even."

"r-r-reckon i know," grumbled toby, as stubborn as he could be; "and i'll b-b-believe it till you p-p-prove the other way."

so, of course, bandy-legs, feeling that he had been challenged, sprung to his feet.

"i'll do it, then, just to show you!" he exclaimed, as he made for the opening of the tent.

a minute later they heard him grumbling and growling within. then his voice came welling forth:

"say, max!"

"hello!"

"was i dreaming, or did i see you put that thing in this haversack?"

"you sure saw me, bandy-legs," replied max, feeling a queer burning sensation dart all over his flesh, as though a suspicion of coming trouble suddenly took possession of him.

"you tucked it away in pink cotton, didn't you?" demanded the one inside the tent.

"that's what he d-d-did," answered toby, before max could speak.

"and say, max, did you take her out again?" asked bandy-legs, reproachfully.

"i did not," answered max, firmly.

he shot a glance toward steve. that individual seemed to be staring, just as the others were. max could discover not the faintest indication on his part of amusement. indeed, he even looked indignant and aroused.

"well, all i c'n say then, is, it's mighty funny," bandy-legs kept on repeating.

"can't you find the little cardboard box?" called out max.

"not any; i tell you it ain't here!" came in reply.

"oh! s-s-shucks! you n-n-need a pair of specs i g-g-guess, bandy!" jeered toby.

"fetch the bag out here," ordered max; and as he was the recognized head of the club, his word in a case of this kind was law.

the broad-shouldered boy quickly hove in sight. he was carrying the leather haversack; and his face seemed puckered up in a frown.

"specs, nothing!" he snapped. "just you ram your paw inside, toby jucklin, and let's see how much better you c'n succeed."

of course, being thus challenged, toby felt in honor bound to make the trial.

everyone watched with rapidly growing interest; and when max stole another look at steve he was more puzzled than before.

was steve trying to play a trick on his chums; or could it be possible that the strong fascination which he admitted pearls always had for him was tempting him to deceive his comrades?

max hated to even allow such a suspicion to gain lodgment in his mind; but after what he had seen, how could he help it?

he determined to say nothing to anyone, not even his cousin owen, but just watch developments.

of course toby's confidence quickly gave way to something akin to dismay. he seemed to rattle the contents of the bag around again and again, but apparently without success.

"well," scoffed bandy-legs, realizing that it was his turn to crow, "why don't you produce the goods, toby? you said i needed specs, didn't you? the first pair we find floating down the big sunflower goes on *your* nose. why don't you show up? let's see that little cardboard box."

toby withdrew his hand.

he seemed about to try and peer within the leather pouch when the voice of max stopped him.

"turn it inside out, toby!" said the leader, quietly.

"yes, dump everything on the table. that's the ticket!"

it was steve himself who said this.

if he was playing a joke steve certainly knew how to keep a straight face. he looked eager, indignant, even alarmed; but max could see not one single sign of secret laughter. even his eyes, those tell-tale orbs by which the secret thoughts are so often betrayed, failed to disclose the twinkle max fully expected to find.

toby obeyed instructions.

quite a motley collection of various things that were apt to prove useful rattled on the rough board table as he held the pouch up by two corners.

the little cardboard box was missing.

toby, as if to make the matter so positive that there could be no mistake, even turned the bag inside out.

"she's gone, fellows!" ejaculated steve, hoarsely. "after all our boasting some sly thief has crept right into our midst, and got away with our little beauty! it's rotten luck, that's what i say. and for the life of me i don't see how he ever did it."

max opened his mouth, as though the temptation to speak was more than he could stand; but he closed it quickly again.

"i'll wait and see what his little game is," he kept saying to himself. "if it's a trick, i never believed steve would be guilty of such a thing. and he's carrying it out just like he meant it, too."

the others were beginning to turn their eyes in the direction of max.

"you've always been such a light sleeper, max; how is it you didn't hear the thief creep in, and search our bag?" bandy-legs asked.

max shrugged his shoulders.

"all i can say, fellows, is that i only woke up once during the night, thinking i heard some one moving about. but i give you my word there was no one in the tent then who didn't belong here."

max was looking straight at steve when he said these words. he really expected to see the other turn red with confusion, perhaps laugh a little, and then in his usual frank way acknowledge that he had taken the pearl just to give his chums a little shock.

to the surprise of max he saw no such sign of guilt upon the face of his friend. apparently, for some reason or other, steve meant to brazen it out.

remembering how the other had seemed to be so strangely fascinated by the handsome pearl, made max shiver a little, he hardly knew why.

"we all saw you put it in the bag, max," declared bandy-legs.

"i tell you what let's do," said owen. "perhaps some fellow is bent on playing a joke on the rest of us. let's settle that point so we won't ever think of it again."

"g-g-good idea, owen. you r-r-run the g-game to suit yourself," piped up the eager toby.

"shall i repeat a form of assertion, max, to which each one of us will subscribe?" asked owen, with his customary readiness.

"certainly; and put it up to me first," replied his cousin.

"then here goes. i hereby affirm that to the best of my knowledge and belief i've neither seen nor handled that little cardboard box containing our pearl since the time max dropped the same in this bag. how is it with you, max; can you truthfully declare the same thing?"

"i can, and hereby do so affirm," replied the other, solemnly.

"bandy-legs, hold up your hand," owen went on.

"sure thing. now put me to the test," flashed the broad-shouldered boy, as he quickly raised his hand.

"the other one, bandy-legs, your right hand. there, that's the ticket. do you solemnly give your word the same as max and myself did, that you haven't seen or handled that little box since it was dropped in this bag by my cousin?"

"i never have," replied the one on the stand.

"toby, how is it with you?" owen kept on.

"i s-s-say exactly the same. so far as i k-know i haven't seen, h-handled or even s-smelled that little b-b-box since max hid it in h-h-here. i'm completely f-f-f-f"-- whistle--"flabbergasted at finding it gone."

"and steve, what about you?" owen asked.

max hastings was more bewildered than ever when he heard the one he had positively see fumbling at the leather bag while the others slept promptly declare:

"so far as i know, fellows, i've never seen or handled that little box since max took it off this table and stuck it in the bag. and that's my sworn affidavy, believe me!"

CHAPTER VI.

the first crop from the river.

after that strange declaration on the part of steve, max felt that his lips must be sealed more than ever.

he wanted a little time to think things over.

besides, max even began to wonder whether he could have just dreamed that he saw steve fumbling at the haversack in the middle of the night, and mumbling to himself all the while.

so he concluded to hold his tongue, say nothing of what he *believed* he had seen, watch steve closely, and wait for new developments to arise.

boys are, as a rule, not much given to long spells of depression.

there is something in the natural buoyancy of a lad's nature that throws off the gloom, and invites the cheery sunlight to enter.

so the whole five were soon eagerly planning as to their work for the day. first of all the two old boats which had served to carry them up to the forks of the evergreen river must be securely hidden. this was mainly on account of those prank-loving boys who, under the leadership of the town bully, ted shafter, they half expected to follow them to this region.

"if they ever came across our boats," declared steve, wrathfully, "you all know what would happen."

"easy enough to smash in the bottoms with a few big dornicks," declared bandy-legs.

"huh! and m-m-make us peg it all the w-w-way b-back to town," grunted toby, who was not known as a great admirer of leg exercise.

"all right, then," said max, promptly; "you and bandy-legs better get busy taking the boats to that big cove where the tall reeds grow so thick. seems to me you ought to be able to hide our craft so well there, the chances of discovery would be next to nothing."

"we c'n do it all right," affirmed bandy-legs, as he started up. "come on, toby, get a move on you."

"wait a minute, c-c-can't you? what's your h-h-hurry. r-r-rome wasn't built in a d-day, i g-g-guess."

"well, go ahead and have it out, because i can see you've got something on your mind. now, what's eating you, toby?" the other complained.

"i only w-wanted to ask max if it wouldn't be g-g-ood p-p-p-p"--whistle--"policy for us to mark the place where we leave the boats. there! do you get that, bandy-legs?"

toby asked this question triumphantly. strange to say, that whenever he stumbled most in his speech, so that he was compelled to halt, and give that short whistle, toby was able to finish what he was saying without a single hitch.

steve often declared it reminded him of a country railroad crossing. there you beheld the warning sign: "stop! look! listen!" and upon complying immediately heard the whistle, after which everything moved on smoothly.

"toby, that's a sensible suggestion of yours," max hastened to declare. "if so be you hide the boats away so well that we couldn't ever find the same again we'd sure be in a nice pickle, eh, owen?"

"i should remark," the one addressed replied; "that tramp to carson would be anything but a peach. and with all our camp stuff to tote along, too."

"excuse me!" bandy-legs exclaimed. "make sure we'll mark the place, boys. now, get a move on, toby. where will we find the rest of you when we get through our job?"

"oh! somewhere around here," max replied. "you see we've got a big job ourselves, taking down the tent, putting it up again some distance away from the water, removing every sign of our having camped here, and then disappearing. you'll be back long before we're done."

his prediction was fulfilled, for when half an hour later toby and his companion showed up, the tent had vanished. steve and owen were carrying blankets, food, and cooking utensils deeper into the woods, while max was working like a beaver close to the water's edge.

"what's going on now, max?" asked bandy-legs, as he watched the actions of his chum.

"i'm doing my best to wipe out all the 'sign' we've made around here," replied max.

"and it looks to me like you're doing a good job of it, too, partner," declared the other, his eyes filled with admiration, as he saw how deftly max smoothed out all traces of where the boats had been pulled up on the pebbly shore of the river.

"oh, well, i'm only a greenhorn at this sort of thing," laughed the busy worker, patting a telltale footprint until it was merged with the surrounding soil; "i'd be reckoned a bungler by any experienced woodsman, you know. but in this case it's an easy job to pull the wool over the eyes of ted and his crowd."

"meaning that they're about as ignorant of all these things as i am?" bandy-legs went on.

"perhaps. but that won't be for long, let me tell you. i'm bound to show you everything i know about these things, and pick up more myself in the bargain. did you get the boats hidden away all right, bandy-legs?"

"gilt-edge, i give you my word. and we tied some of the reeds together near the spot. only a feller who was lookin' for the tag'd notice where we did it. toby or me, why we could go straight to the spot, with only one eye open."

"all right. then suppose you get busy helping steve and owen. nobody must step back here again to leave fresh tracks after i've rubbed these all out."

max continued to work as steadily as a beaver. step by step he retreated backward, removing all traces left by the campers.

it was an arduous task, especially when he came to where the tent and fire had stood. but really the boy proved to have a natural talent for this sort of thing. he utterly removed all the ashes, scattered some brush over the spot, and at the end of an hour max stood on the border of the dense woods casting a last careful look over the field of his recent labors.

"i ought to pat myself on the back over that job," he chuckled; "and it wouldn't be throwing any bouquets either. ten to one ted shafter and his gang could land here, cook a meal, and lie around, without ever once dreaming we'd spent a night on the same camp ground."

then he withdrew from the scene of his recent operations.

picking his way through the woods, after a time he heard voices, and then discovered the tent.

the new camp site had been selected by owen, and it certainly did him credit. max stood for a few minutes watching his chums work, and smiling with pleasure over the prospect of a full week or more in that delightful secluded spot.

trees grew densely around the place, and until one drew very near, it was next to impossible to discover the dingy old waterproof tent that nestled in the midst of the thick undergrowth.

a clear little gurgling spring sang close by, affording all the water they would need for drinking and cooking purposes.

but, as max stood and looked, the happy smile gradually left his face, to be succeeded by an expression of grave concern.

as he was watching the movements of steve at the time, it could be easily understood what pressed upon his mind.

"oh, come, this won't do at all," max presently muttered, pressing his teeth together resolutely. "it's all going to come out right, sooner or later. of course it looks mighty queer just now, and i can't for the life of me understand it; but i've known steve all my life, and he's never yet been called a *thief!* i'll just bottle up, and hold my horses, and watch what he does, because i'm bound to find out."

so he strode into the new camp, walking all around, and quite free with his hearty compliments concerning the fine way owen and steve had done their part of the business.

"but looky here," burst out the impatient steve, after a while, "we're wasting time, you know. some of us might as well be up the river gathering a few pecks of mussels."

"t-t-that's so," declared toby. "and it's up to max to s-s-say who goes out f-f-first."

"suppose, then, steve and myself lead off, and make the first try," max suggested. he had a double object in nominating steve as his working partner on this occasion. in the first place he knew the impatient nature of the fiery lad, and that his heart was more set upon the finding of other pearls like unto the lost one than any of the others.

this was not all.

having steve in his company for a couple of hours would give max a good chance to study the other closely.

perhaps, too, if steve were really playing a practical joke on his comrades he might, without meaning to do so, let a hint drop that would serve to betray the object he had in view.

"here, don't forget the bags we fetched along to carry the mussels in," said bandy-legs.

"and i h-h-hope i g-g-get a chance to make a t-t-try this afternoon," remarked toby, not a little disappointed because he had been passed over when max selected the one to accompany him on the first hunting expedition.

so the two boys walked off, taking with them a couple of bags. max also thought it wise to shoulder the reliable old shotgun.

"it isn't the game season, i know," he said, as the others looked their surprise, "and about the only thing we ought to shoot right now would be woodcock. i saw a marsh where i reckon i'll find some of the long-billed mud diggers. you know they get their food by sticking their bills deep down in the mud. that's why you always look for woodcock in a wet spot or marsh. ready, steve? all right, we'll make another start."

about twenty minutes later the two boys had reached the bank of the little river, half a mile or so above their first camp site.

they lost no time, but set to work at once, removing shoes and socks, and rolling the legs of their trowsers above their knees.

then, with selected, sharp-pointed sticks, after wading into the shallow water, they began to poke carefully around in all such promising places as mussels would most likely be found.

steve gave the first triumphant cry.

"i've got one, max! and say, he's just a jim-dandy big fellow, too, believe me! now, i wonder if he's going to present us with the mate of that little beauty of a pearl we lost so queerly."

max was watching his chum closely.

"he says that just as naturally as if he meant every word of it," the boy muttered; puzzled more than ever; and then raising his voice he went on to say: "you'll just have to take it out in guessing, then, old chap, because we can't bother stopping to open every find we come across."

"i should say not," replied steve, and immediately added: "hey! what d'ye think, here's another of the blessed old shellfish, just poking his nose out of the sand like he wanted to invite me to gather him in."

"good enough! i haven't picked up my first one yet; and here you're walking away from me double-quick. guess i'd better get busy."

the truth was max had been so wrapped up in watching his chum that as yet he had hardly tried to make a find.

but he now set industriously to work. there were times when the mussels came in fast; and again they seemed to fall off.

gradually the boys worked up-stream, crossing and recrossing as they searched.

"we're covering the ground all right," asserted steve, as his laugh announced another prize; "and believe me, we clean 'em out as we go. how many have you got in your bag, max?"

"about nine or ten, i reckon, steve."

"i've got fourteen, and some busters among 'em. i'll be pretty badly disappointed if one out of the lot don't turn out a good milk-white pearl," the other called out.

"perhaps it'd be better not to mention that word so loud again, steve," cautioned the other.

"are you saying that just on general principles like, max, or is there a reason?" and steve, as he made this demand, splashed closer to his chum.

"oh, well!" max went on, "you know they say that sometimes even the trees and rocks have ears. and we don't know who might be hiding around, watching us right now."

"did you see or hear anything to make you think that way?" asked the nervous steve.

"can't say i did," replied max; "but i thought it good policy to sling my gun over my back by the strap, and not leave it ashore. sorry now i brought it along; but we don't want it stolen like our pearl was."

"that's right, we don't," asserted steve, without the slightest hesitation. "if these shell gatherers have got the nerve to sneak into our tent and make way with our first pearl, i reckon they wouldn't hold back at taking a good old scatter-gun that chanced to be lying around loose."

"let's get busy again, steve."

"right-o! i'd like to make my score an even two dozen before we meander back to camp for lunch. and i s'pose the other feller's 'll want to have a try next time. anyhow, you and me can be amusing ourselves opening these mossbacks, and finding out what's inside."

half an hour later max called a halt. as steve had only twenty-three mussels in his bag he did hate to give up the work the worst kind; but the demands of his appetite made him willing to return to the camp.

"they're heavy enough to tote along," steve admitted when almost there. "and, after all, you had no use for your gun, max."

"i'll slip over to the marsh this p. m., and see what luck i can have," returned the other.

"there's the camp, with owen cooking dinner. but look at bandy-legs, would you, max? he sure acts as if he'd run up against some hard nut to crack!"

CHAPTER VII.

bandy-legs wants to know.

"say, i wonder what next is going to disappear around this old camp?" bandy-legs was saying in a disgusted tone, as the two who had been over to the river drew near.

"why, what do you miss now?" asked max.

"you remember that old cap we found last night?" the other went on.

"why of course i do," max replied. "do you mean to say you kept it?"

"well, i had an idea i'd give it back to the poor feller if ever we ran across him," bandy-legs continued, for he was really a warm-hearted boy, as his chums well knew; "and when we came here to this new camp i remember as plain as anything sticking that same old cap on the end of this bush that grows to a point. then just now i noticed it was gone."

"that's as sure as the nose on your face, bandy-legs," remarked steve.

"now don't you go to making fun of my nose," the other retorted. "it's a good, honest nose, if it is big. and it never yet made a habit of sticking itself in other people's business. that's the way with all griffin noses; they mind their own affairs every time."

max knew there was danger of an argument, because steve was likely to take this as a challenge. therefore, to promote peace, max thrust himself between the other two.

"have you asked owen and toby about it?" he inquired of bandy-legs.

"sure i did, right away," came the answer.

"and they denied touching it?" max went on, determined to sift the matter down, trifling though it might appear to be at first sight.

"both of 'em declared they'd never even been near this same old bush," the other replied.

"that looks queer," steve broke in.

"owen did say he saw the old cap just where i stuck it," bandy-legs continued.

"how long ago, owen?" demanded max.

"oh, i should say half an hour or so. i happened to look that way and got quite a start, because at first i thought it was somebody watching us. then when i saw how bandy-legs had fixed it on the bush i had to laugh."

"mebbe the wind carried it away," suggested steve.

"that's so; i never once thought of that," ejaculated the puzzled one, eagerly clutching at a straw that promised to explain the mystery.

"how about it, max?" asked steve.

"well, your idea sounds all right, steve, but unfortunately it has one weak place."

"as what, now?" asked bandy-legs. "why, there hasn't been a breath of wind all the morning," max went on, with a chuckle. "i remember wishing it would come up, for the sun was sure something fierce when we were wading about, looking for clams."

"you're right, max," called out owen, who could easily hear all that was said, "no breeze ever carried that cap away, and i know it."

"what did, then?" demanded bandy-legs, bent on getting some sort of solution to the puzzle.

"this old country must be hoaxed or bewitched, i guess," grumbled steve. "things just seem able to disappear without anybody taking 'em. first we had to lose our bully little pearl that just took my eye; and now even a ragged old cap has to walk off by itself."

"oh, not quite so bad as that, i think, steve," max laughed as he said this. "when that cap went away it was through the agency of legs, according to my notion."

"oh, i see now what max means!" cried bandy-legs; "he believes some gay old mother squirrel just took a notion to line her nest with that ragged cap, and made off with it."

41

"rats!" exclaimed steve; "max don't think anything of the kind. see him examining the ground right now, will you? i reckon he thinks that same runt of a boy came back after his cap, and got it, too, in the bargain."

at that max laughed aloud.

"good guess, steve, old chap. that's just what happened, and if you look where i point, all of you can see the same small footprint we found last night where the old cap lay."

"he's right, fellows, for here it is!" cried steve.

they all had to crowd around for a look, although max warned them to be careful, so that the impression of the boy's ragged shoe might not be trodden upon.

"well, just to t-t-think what b-b-bright fellers we are," said toby, in apparent disgust; "when even a r-r-runt of a boy c'n steal up and s-s-spy on us without a b-b-blessed one knowing it."

"huh!" grunted bandy-legs, who seemed in a peculiar frame of mind for one who was usually so good natured, "who's got a better right to that cap, i'd like to know, than the boy that owns it. put yourself in his place, toby, and tell me if you wouldn't just grab your own cap if you saw it? course you would--we all would, and i don't blame the kid a little bit."

"too bad he didn't like the looks of our crowd," steve remarked.

"what makes you think he didn't?" owen asked, smiling.

"well, he acted like he was afraid of us," replied steve.

"t-t-tell you what, boys, i reckon it wasn't our looks, after all, that s-s-scared him, though bandy-legs does resemble a terrible p-p-pirate when he wears that old zebra s-s-sweater of his."

"then what did?" demanded the one who had been thus picked out as a special mark, while he ran a hand fondly up and down the sleeve of the white-and-black striped garment, worn in spite of the heat of the day.

"our g-g-guns!" broke out toby triumphantly.

"that's a good guess, toby," remarked max. "perhaps the boy believes we're some sort of deputy sheriffs, and up here to give the man he's with trouble. anyhow, i have a pretty good idea myself that it was our guns that made him so shy."

"all right," remarked steve, "the pitcher may go to the well once too often. you mark my words, if he keeps on sniffing around our camp much longer he'll get caught."

"sure he will," echoed bandy-legs, grimly. "we want that pearl back, don't we. boys?"

"and we're going to have it, too," observed another of the group, in a positive way.

max had that queer feeling pass over him again; for it was steve who made this half-angry remark.

what could it mean?

he had always believed steve to be as honest as the day was long, his only faults being a hasty temper, and a desire to do things without sufficient preparation.

but that the boy would deliberately *steal*, simply because he happened to be fascinated by the beauty of the pearl, seemed beyond belief.

no wonder, then, that the bewildered max sighed, and rubbed his eyes with his knuckles, as though hardly knowing whether he were awake or asleep.

as nothing more could be done, the five boys adjourned to the camp, where owen quickly completed his preparations for lunch. they had decided to have the heavy meal, called dinner, in the evening, so that the work of the day might not be interfered with.

when those who had been off hunting shellfish had returned, tired with their labors, it would be nice to gather around, and take their time in enjoying the bountiful meal that had been prepared by the cook appointed for that day.

each of them expected to take a hand at this necessary job. in anticipation of the opportunity to shine as a talented *chef* bandy-legs had in secret been coaxing the hired girl at home to teach him a lot of things.

as his turn would come on the second day, he could hardly restrain his impatience. he surely calculated that when his chums saw what wonderful things *real talent* could accomplish, they would easily vote him a prize.

but bandy-legs had much to learn.

his ambition was all right, but he would soon discover the vast difference between cooking at a gas range or the family coal stove and trying to accomplish the same result out in the wilds over an open wood fire.

then, again, he had stuffed his head so very full of different recipes that the chances were poor bandy-legs must get the formulas mixed, which would result in some mighty queer messes to be tried upon his patient campmates.

after the meal was finished those who were to do the grand wading act of the afternoon got ready to go forth.

they took the bags, and received minute directions from max concerning the best way for finding the mussels, half buried as they were in mud or sand.

max also made a rude map on paper, taking in the supposed course of the winding river, as well as the country that came between.

"here you can see the trail i've marked as the shortest cut to camp," he finished, pointing to a dotted line that seemed to be almost straight. "it runs exactly southwest, you notice, boys."

"but how are we going to always know what *is* southwest?" asked bandy-legs, receiving the chart.

at that toby gave a snort of disdain.

"w-w-what d'ye s'pose this is for, s-s-silly?" he demanded, dangling a little nickel-plated object before the eyes of his companion.

"that's right, we're going to have the bully little compass along with us," declared the doubting one, looking considerably relieved; for truth to tell, if bandy-legs feared any one thing more than another, it was the haunting idea of being lost in a great big wilderness, and meeting a slow and dreadful death through starvation.

"and even if we should l-l-lose this useful t-t-trinket," continued toby, exultantly, "i'd know how to t-t-tell which was north, all right."

"huh! why, of course, by the moss on the sides of the trees," observed bandy-legs. "guess i heard max tell that, all right. never forget it, either. but how the dickens is a feller to ever remember *which* side of the big trees this moss always grows on?"

"stop and think," said max, who had an idea that some day this information might be useful to his chum; "the hard storms of winter generally come out of the northwest, don't they?"

"reckon you're right; though to tell the truth i'd never noticed it much," bandy-legs replied.

"well, you want to wake up and notice everything that happens," advised max, seriously. "it's the fellow who keeps awake, and sees and hears it all, that gets on in this world, bandy-legs. and you know it, too."

"sure. i know my weak points, max; and the best thing about me is the fact that i want to wake up and do better. but about that moss--does it always grow exactly on the sides of the trees pointing toward the northwest?"

"in the majority of cases," replied the other; "here and there it may vary some, but anybody with half an eye can decide the right direction. then in the night you have the north star, which you know can always be found by drawing an imaginary straight line along the two stars forming the end of the bowl of the dipper, generally called the great bear."

"oh! that's easy. but once i heard you say a common ordinary watch could be made to serve as a compass; how about that, max?" added bandy-legs, showing considerable interest in the subject.

"so it can, but i'll explain that at another time. you fellows had better be moving now," and max turned his back on the other as the best way to shut him off; for bandy-legs was a great questioner.

"so-long!" called out toby, cheerfully, as he started to follow the trail left by max and steve on their way from the river, half a mile away.

"if we meet up with this mysterious shell gatherer, what ought we to do?" asked the second boy, halting.

"act friendly, and pay attention to your own business, that's all. nobody will hurt you," max called out, as he turned into the camp.

CHAPTER VIII.

a great find.

"when do we begin, max?"

steve asked this question a short time after the three left in the camp had cleaned up the tin pans used in preparing and eating the warm meal, and owen had gone off to try and secure a mess of bass for supper.

steve had been usually fast in his share of the work, even for him. max had noticed this fact, and could give a good guess as to what was spurring the other on to such exertions.

"begin what?" he asked, as if in dense ignorance.

"why, in opening our catch, you know," steve replied, jerking his thumb to where the little pile of mussels lay, close by the camp fire.

steve had himself emptied the two bags, upon their arrival in camp. evidently he did not mean to take any chances of having the precious bivalves stolen by the prowling half-grown wild boy. and in order to provide against such a catastrophe he had been very careful to deposit their morning's "catch" in an open spot so destitute of shrubbery that no one could approach within ten feet unseen.

max smiled.

truth to tell he was a little eager himself to set to work investigating the insides of these shells.

the remarkable luck attending their first attempt gave him more or less hope that other prizes might crop up to reward their continued efforts.

and the outing boys had outlined such a glorious programme for the long vacation, if only they could raise the large amount of money needed to carry out their ardent plans, that naturally max was heart and soul interested in the result.

besides, max had a half-formed resolution that if luck favored them, so that they found another pearl, he would set a trap that very evening. he was burning with eager curiosity to discover whether steve might repeat his strange action of the preceding night. and in case this happened, max was grimly resolved to settle the matter once and for all by clutching hold of the other while in the act.

"oh! you're wondering whether we're going to find anything in that lot; is that it!" max remarked, as he picked up an old oyster knife he had carried along for the purpose of prying open the mussels, no easy task for greenhorns at the business, as the boys' cut fingers already testified.

"you just bet i am," returned steve, possessing himself of the heavy kitchen knife. "come along and let's see if we had our wading and toting the find all the way to camp for nothing."

"just as you say," max continued.

"what d'ye take that kettle for!" asked steve.

"to hold the mussels as we get 'em out. let the meat and juice drop in here. then we'll examine the whole thing several times for results. and don't forget, both toby and bandy-legs made us promise to have a mess of these same fresh-water clams cooked for supper."

so, taking the vessel and the much-used oyster knife, max squatted on the ground tailor fashion alongside the pile of shellfish.

both of them set to work, max calmly, as was his wont, but steve showing the greatest nervousness.

finding that his method of trying to open the stubborn bivalves was awkward, as they could not be handled like oysters, max took a second knife. placing the mussel in an upright position he would drive the blade down between the two shells by giving it several sharp taps with a piece of wood. when the stubborn mussel finally yielded to this treatment max was able to turn back one shell, and then scrape out the entire contents of the other.

a dozen had been opened presently, and so far as they could see, there was not a sign of a pearl, large or small.

steve's disappointment made itself manifest in the look that gradually crept over his face.

"guess we've drawn a blank this time, max," he remarked, when the seventeenth bivalve failed to yield up any gleaming little milk-white prize.

"oh! that isn't a dead sure thing," replied the other, never ready to yield his hopeful spirit, "this is a lottery, you know. the pearls are to be found. we know that, steve, by our first success. if not in this lot, perhaps in what our chums bring later. there are other days to follow; and we're bound to put in a week trying our luck."

that was the sort of talk to buoy up steve's spirits. he was always an impulsive chap, and had often been called "touch-and-go steve," because of his quick temper. it had many times carried him into serious trouble, though, as is usually the case with these impetuous fellows, steve always quickly repented of his wrath, and was apt to apologize.

"here goes for the eighteenth," he remarked, picking up another mussel, and setting to work industriously.

"this is a scrawny looking one, and i just reckon it'll be time wasted," he added.

"you never can tell," laughed max, himself busily engaged.

"that's so," steve went on; "because they do say these precious little pearls are manufactured by the oyster or mussel to cover up some gritty object that has managed to work into the shell, and which they just can't eject."

"yes, that's the accepted theory," max asserted.

"when i read that, i remember figuring out how a smart genius might make a few millions," remarked steve.

"you mean by introducing the same kind of grit in some hundreds of shellfish, and making the things work up a lot of fine pearls, eh, steve?"

"that's what. don't you think it could be done, max?"

"well, i've heard it's been tried, but since the price of pearls has advanced all the while, i guess the success of the experiment wasn't so much," the other went on to say, as he bent his head down quickly to scrutinize the contents of his opened shell.

"oh!" gasped steve, catching his breath.

"what's the matter?" asked max, his own voice as steady and calm as ever.

"looky here, will you, max--ain't that a beaut, though?"

the excited steve managed to pluck some small object out of the opened shell he held, though his fingers trembled like the quivering leaves of an aspen.

when he placed this in the palm of his hand it was seen to be a lovely little milk-white pearl, nearly half the size of a buckshot.

"that looks good to me," remarked max. "just as fine as the one we lost, eh, steve?"

"you bet it is; and we'll make sure no thief lays hands on this beauty, max," replied the delighted finder of the new treasure.

"now, suppose, just for luck, i took a notion to go you one better," chuckled max.

"hey! what d'ye mean?" exclaimed his chum. "have you been shaking hands with good luck as well as me? open up, and show what you've got." "shut your eyes, and count five," laughed max; "now look, and see what i found."

"my goodness gracious; why, it's half again as big as my find; a regular jim-dandy pearl, max," cried steve, trembling all over with, eager delight, as his enraptured eyes fell upon the object max exposed.

"yes, much larger, i admit," the other went on to say with due deliberation; "but not quite so perfect in form. your pearl might prove to be the more valuable one when it came to selling them."

"oh! just to think of it, max, we've got two already," steve remarked as he took both the prizes in his hand, and surveyed them with that wistful look in his eyes; for, as he had more than once admitted, pearls always had a peculiar fascination for him.

max was watching his companion's face closely, trying to read the emotions that chased each other across steve's features.

"yes, and the chance is still open," he said, slowly.

"meaning that we may find a lot more; is that it, max?" steve demanded.

"who can say? it's a lottery all around. the next mussel might give us another prize. then, again, perhaps we'll clean out the stream and never get any reward."

max had a way of looking things squarely in the face. he seldom allowed his enthusiasm to get the better of his calm, deliberate judgment. and consequently he did not suffer the grievous disappointment that came so frequently to excitable steve.

"anyway, we ought to get quite a bunch of money for these two dandy gems," steve remarked.

"i wouldn't be surprised at all," max assented.

"what d'ye think they're worth, max?"

"well, now, that's where you get me. i'm as green as the next one when it comes to putting a value on pearls. only an expert can tell that," the other quickly replied.

"shucks! but you can give a guess, can't you?" persisted steve, not to be wholly disappointed.

"it would have to be a wide one, then, steve."

"all right; let's have it!" observed the other.

"well, i don't doubt but what we'll be able to sell each of these pearls for a hundred apiece," max asserted.

"dollars, you mean, max?"

"sure thing. and perhaps they may bring us five or ten times as much. i'll have my father take them to the city, and consult an expert," max went on.

"wow! that's going some, now, i tell you!" cried the other, with delight pictured on his glowing face.

"two hundred sure, first pop, and mebbe a thousand! say, max, it begins to look like our wildest dreams might come true, and we'll be able to carry out all those bully old plans we made."

"yes," said max, deliberately, "if we can only guard our new find better than we did the other."

"we must make sure to have one chum doing sentry duty all the time," remarked steve, solemnly. "that's only good sound sense, i take it, max."

"guess you're right about that, my boy," asserted the other, with a peculiar little smile that, however, steve failed to notice. "and, now, suppose we finish up the lot we've still got to open." "right you are," declared steve.

"but, first, please let me have those pearls. i'd hate to have them lost in this grass here. and i believe i can keep them safe in this red handkerchief of mine till we find a chance to stow 'em away in the haversack, after the boys examine our find."

"in the haversack!" echoed steve. "why, that's where we had the one that disappeared, box and all."

"sure thing," max asserted.

"but think of the risk--" steve began.

"oh, we've got to hide 'em *somewhere*, you know," laughed max; "and they say lightning never strikes in the same place twice. besides, you forget that we expect to post a sentry, so that your eyes, or mine, or those of owen, toby or bandy-legs, will be on the bag all through the night. i'll take the pearls now, please."

steve somehow seemed a little loth about letting the lovely little gems pass out of his possession.

as he handed them over, his chum plainly heard him give a sigh; and he caught him repeating the words:

"in the haversack, and we've got to look out."

then both of the boys set to work.

the remaining shellfish were soon opened, and although the young pearl seekers searched eagerly, with hope tugging at their hearts, no new prize rewarded their efforts.

"the queerest thing of all," remarked steve, after he had mastered his disappointment, "was in our finding the pair of beauties at the same time."

"yes, and i believe my mussel was as thin and scrawny looking a fellow as the one you complained of," laughed max.

"forget that, please," remarked his chum, with a grimace. "and just to think, i came near throwing that consumptive looking one away as worthless. it's taught me a lesson, sure, max."

"yes, and one you'll never forget, eh, steve?"

"i never will," declared the other, vehemently. "whenever i think of this lucky strike i'm going to understand that you never can judge things, people also, by outside looks."

"sometimes the finest gems come in the meanest of coverings, you mean, eh, steve?"

"right-o. and now what'll we do?" asked the other.

"carry the shells away, because in a few days we'd object to the rank odor so near our tent. listen, steve. make a heap of the things, under some tree you can remember well. we can call that our shell pile, you know."

"see here, you've got a meaning back of all that, you know it," complained steve.

max laughed aloud.

"how smart we're getting, old chap," he remarked. "but between us i don't mind saying that i'm curious to see what will happen."

"that is, you mean to give *some one* a good chance to get away with all these mussel shells, if so be they feel inclined, eh, max."

max nodded his head in the affirmative.

"meaning this man and boy who seem to be hiding out up here, just like they were afraid to be seen, and employing their time in raking in all the scattered shells left by the muskrats and 'coons--how about that, max?" steve continued, as he gathered the opened shells in an extra bag, preparatory to removing them.

"you hit the nail on the head when you say that, steve. they seem to know the mother-of-pearl inside lining of the shells will bring in some money. and i reckon they're piling the shells up in some cave or secret place, meaning to get them down the river in a dugout canoe sooner or later."

"well, they're welcome to all the shells we gather," remarked steve, with a shake of the head; "but they'd better not try to steal any more of our pearls, that's what"; and so saying he marched off with his load, leaving max more sadly puzzled than ever.

CHAPTER IX.

max wonders still more.

the afternoon wore on.

steve kept busy doing things until owen turned up with a mess of perch, the bass declining to take his worm bait.

then the story of the find had to be gone over again, and the prizes exhibited. owen was just as much pleased as the others, and declared that it began to look as though the best of their dreams had a chance of coming true.

"i think i saw that boy, come to mention it," owen remarked, after they had talked over the splendid good luck that had fallen to their lot, until the subject was pretty well exhausted.

"how did that happen?" asked max.

"did you get a chance to talk with him, and ask him why he grabbed our pearl?" demanded steve.

"oh! not much," chuckled owen. "fact is, he seemed pretty much like a scared rabbit. first thing i knew he was staring at me over a bunch of brush. then he turned and scooted off like fun."

"but you called out to him, didn't you?" asked steve.

"of course, but it only seemed to make him fly the faster. say, he's a sprinter, all right. that fellow could get down to second base before the ball seven times out of seven, i don't care who the catcher was," owen went on to say, positively.

"then you couldn't catch him?" asked max, in a disappointed tone.

"huh! guess i didn't even start, after i saw what he could put up in the running line. besides," owen went on to say, "you must remember that i was tired, and carrying my fishing rod, as well as a bully old string of perch, which i calculated to clean for supper. then, i hadn't lost any boy, you see. so i just hollered after him, and tried to let the silly goose know we didn't mean to hurt him."

"but it was no go?" remarked steve.

"oh! he turned to look back a few times, but all the same he disappeared from sight. perhaps next time he won't be quite so frightened," owen observed.

"there may be some reason for it we don't know about," suggested max.

"you mean that they don't want people to know about their collecting these shells, for fear that their little business might be broken up?" steve asked.

"that's one reason why they'd try to hide things," max admitted, "but there might be another. i spoke of it before, you may remember, boys?"

"sure you did, max," declared steve, quickly; "and mebbe you hit the bullseye when you said this man might be hiding out up here--that p'r'aps he'd gone and done something to break the law; and when he saw our guns he expected we might be sent by the sheriff to arrest him."

"i still stick to that idea," max declared; "but we may know the truth sooner or later. one thing we must do if ever we get the chance, and that is let these shell gatherers know we don't mean to harm 'em even a little bit."

"but they've just got to let our pearls be, or else they're going to get into trouble, that's what," remarked the pugnacious steve, with a determined shake of his head and a gritting of his teeth.

max saw and heard, and was more deeply bewildered than ever. he could not for the life of him understand such contrary actions on the part of steve.

max could positively declare that he had seen steve taking something from the haversack on the preceding night, when their first prize pearl vanished so mysteriously; and yet here he was apparently aroused over their loss, and denouncing the thief with greater vim than any of the rest.

"but i'm bound to find out what it all means," max consoled himself by saying over and over. "if it takes all summer i'll fight it out on this line, like grant did in the battles of the wilderness. steve acts like he was innocent; but i guess i've got a pair of good eyes, and it was *him* i saw fumbling at the haversack, all right."

it had been the intention of max to try and find a few woodcock in the wet ground of the marsh.

other things coming up caused him to put this project off until another day. it was really no time for hunting, with a hot sun beaming down. perhaps later on he might find plenty of chances to indulge in his favorite sport.

owen had cleaned his catch, and supper was being started when voices were heard approaching.

"here comes toby and bandy-legs," sang out steve, who had at the first sound made as if to reach for the guns that rested against the tree close to the opening of the tent.

"well," remarked owen, looking up, "it's good to know they didn't go and get lost, anyhow. perhaps that compass kept 'em from straying out of the trail you said you made, max?"

"huh! we made it so plain," remarked steve. "that a baby ought to be able to follow our tracks. but then toby and bandy-legs always seem to tumble into trouble if there's just half a chance to get mixed up. say, they've got the bags pretty well filled up with mussels, anyhow."

"you bet we have," panted bandy-legs, as he set his burden down.

"g-g-great s-s-sport," remarked toby, following.

"glad you like it," laughed max, "because we expect to do a heap of wading while we're up here."

"d-d-did you open the others?"

"we sure did," chuckled steve.

"f-f-find anything in 'em?"

"did we? say, show up, max; give these poor tired fellows a peek, that'll make 'em forget all their troubles." and steve grinned happily as he watched the other deliberately take out his bandana, unroll its folds, and then disclose to the wondering eyes of toby and bandy-legs the two lovely white pearls that snuggled against the red background.

"whoop!" gurgled bandy-legs, excitedly, his eyes round with wonder and delight.

toby on his part became so excited that for the time being he could not say a word. his breath came in gasps, and his lips moved vainly as he tried to express his feelings. finally, after steve had pounded him on the back a few times, poor toby managed to pucker up his lips and emit the customary sharp whistle which seemed to act like magic upon his overwrought feelings, just as the safety brake does with a runaway car.

then he drew in a long breath, and enunciated, as plainly and clearly as max himself could have done, the one significant word:

"bully!"

"gee whiz! i guess i'll get busy right away," remarked bandy-legs, eagerly.

"no need," spoke up owen. "your turn will come to-morrow. i'm serving as cook this afternoon. don't you smell fish frying? i've been over to the river myself and hooked a bunch of nice perch."

"f-f-fine. g-g-good for you, owen," said toby, slapping the other on the back.

"oh, shucks! i didn't have any idea of wanting to knock you out of a job, old fellow. where's that oyster knife, max?" asked the returned pearl hunter.

"say, he wants to begin opening his catch right away," remarked steve. "and i'll have to show him how we did it, max."

this he proceeded to do with alacrity, and the three were soon busily engaged. bandy-legs proved more or less clumsy, and not only cut himself several times on the sharp edges of the shells, but banged his fingers with the heavy stick with which he pounded.

but one way or another by degrees every one of the mussels were opened.

disappointment followed, for while three pearls were discovered two were so small as to give but little promise of returns; while the third proved to be irregular in shape.

"never mind," said max, when he learned the result of the hunt. "better luck to-morrow. we've fared splendidly already. and we know our scheme is going to be a success. cheer up. there's owen calling us to supper. and we can eat our catch as long as it tastes good to us. draw around, fellows, and sample our new cook's stuff."

the five boys were soon engaged in satisfying the cravings of hunger. and through the nearby woods crept the appetizing odors of coffee and fried fish that must have been very tantalizing to any prowler less fortunate than themselves.

CHAPTER X.

at dead of night.

so the night found them.

toby and bandy-legs had managed to recover from their keen disappointment over the poor result of their afternoon's work.

"reckon we must have struck a bad place," the latter remarked, as they all lounged around the cheery fire after supper had been finished.

"that's a f-f-fact," commented toby, nodding his head in a wise fashion; "i've read that these p-p-pearls happen in a q-q-queer way. f-f-find 'em all in a h-h-heap, and then nothin' doin' for w-w-weeks."

"then our chums must have struck the jolliest place on the whole river," bandy-legs observed.

"h-h-hope they m-m-marked it, then," toby went on.

"how about it, max, steve?" demanded the other pearl hunter of the afternoon.

"sure we did," grunted steve, who somehow seemed strangely quiet for him, a fact that gave max considerable uneasiness, knowing what he did.

"and i remember telling you where we did most of our tramping in the water," he observed.

toby grinned rather foolishly.

"g-g-guess that's so," he admitted.

"yes," spoke up bandy-legs, "but you see we expected that you'd cleaned out that place pretty well; and as we wanted to pick up a good load we went higher up."

"that's where you made the mistake, then," remarked owen. "perhaps max and steve located something like a pocket. if i take a turn in the morning i believe i'll go over all the ground they did and pick up a few shells."

"i'll go along to show you if you say so," steve suggested.

"how about it, max?" inquired owen.

"call it settled at that," came the ready response.

they talked and compared notes, and laid plans for the glorious future, as the cheery fire crackled and the hour grew later.

max had shaped the little scheme he had in mind.

the pearls were supposed to be safely lodged in a tiny packet which he had placed in the haversack in the presence of all the others.

this, however, was all a delusion and a snare, for in pursuance of his plans max had secretly managed to quietly slip the two really valuable gems into his pocket, where he afterwards made them secure.

all this was done with a definite object in view, for he more than half expected that before another dawn came the haversack would be visited again.

by degrees the boys fell away, since max had plainly announced that he would take the first watch.

no one seemed disposed to dispute the honor with him, because they were all very sleepy.

first toby crawled under the tent, and by his heavy breathing they knew he was dead to the world.

next steve followed suit, and then bandy-legs.

"wake me early, mother dear, because to-morrow will be the first of may," the latter sang out, as he vanished.

this left only max and owen.

now, the weight of his secret was weighing so heavily upon max that he had made up his mind to take owen into his confidence should a good chance arise.

it seemed to be on hand.

accordingly, after binding his cousin to secrecy, max began to relate the strange thing he had seen on the preceding night.

of course owen was properly shocked.

he, too, had the utmost confidence in steve dowdy, and found great difficulty in believing that the other could ever descend to such a low state as making a thief out of himself.

"the plaguy pearls must have fairly turned his head, max," he declared, with almost savage earnestness.

"just what i was beginning to believe," the other admitted, with a shake of his head.

"but what can we do about it, max?"

"i'm going to watch," replied the other.

"to-night, you mean?"

"yes, the fever is still in steve's veins. he doesn't seem to act like himself. and, owen, d'ye know, i've read somewhere that some people are strangely affected by certain kinds of gems. they seem bewitched when looking at or handling the same."

"that's it, max. pearls must have some sort of terrible fascination for poor steve."

"he admitted as much himself, and you all heard him say so," declared max.

"all right, count me in," owen went on.

"what d'ye mean by saying that, cousin?" asked max.

"only that you won't have to watch alone, max."

"just as you say, my boy. glad to have your company. but we'd better be making preparations to keep our eyes on that bag," max went on.

"why, i can see it from here, so long as the fire keeps blazing," owen asserted.

"i purposely hung it in that place, and drew back the tent flap so i could keep an eye on the bag all the time. so owen, let's settle down here, and make ourselves as comfy as we can."

"all we have to do is to drop a little wood on the fire once in a while, eh, max?"

"that's right; and while we watch we can talk in whispers if we feel like it, owen."

"still, it would be better to keep quiet, i suppose," suggested the cousin of max.

"of course. he might hear us, and lie low," replied the one who was engineering things.

"but you've fixed it so that while we lie here on our blankets, no one would be apt to notice us from the tent. you had a purpose in doing that, i expect?" questioned owen.

"i thought he might take a look around first to see where i was; and not discovering me in sight would believe i had gone to sleep on my post," max went on.

"this is a nightmare of a time," grumbled owen.

"that's right," echoed the other, promptly. "seems to me i must be dreaming when i find myself suspecting steve of such a nasty thing. but wait up and see, owen. if nothing happens i'll be surprised, likewise mighty well pleased."

they accordingly lapsed into silence.

minutes glided by. to both the boys they seemed to be shod with lead, so slowly did the time pass.

when the fire burned low, as it did on several occasions, max would crawl out, manage to toss an armful of wood upon the red embers, and immediately seek his hiding place again.

one, two hours had gone, and so far nothing out of the common had come to pass.

owen found himself getting somewhat sleepy, and in various ways he fought against the drowsy sensation.

"that's an owl, i reckon, ain't it, max?" he whispered when certain queer sounds floated to their ears out of the depths of the forest.

"of course," replied the other, in the same cautious tone, which could not have been heard ten feet away.

"and those are tree frogs croaking close by?" continued owen, who knew all about these things from reading; while his cousin did the same through practical experience.

60

"they're calling for more rain!" chuckled max; "but i hope the old fellow up above, who turns on the sprinkler when he takes a notion, don't pay any attention, because rain in camp is generally a nasty time."

once more the two boys lapsed into silence.

perhaps another half hour had passed when owen, whose eyes were getting very heavy, so that he found himself nodding, felt something touch his arm.

he started violently, possibly under the impression that some snake or wild animal from the woods had reached them unawares.

"h-s-sh!"

why, to be sure, it was max who hissed this warning in his ear. and, of course, it must be his cousin's hand that was laid on his own arm.

"look!"

the one word proved sufficient to make owen remember what they were lying there for. accordingly he craned his neck so as to see the interior of the tent.

the fire was burning fairly well, and as max had fastened the canvas flaps unusually far back, in order to admit plenty of air, as he had said at the time, it was easy to see.

owen felt another thrill, immediately succeeded by a chilly sensation.

there was a movement within the tent, as if some person might be advancing toward the spot where the haversack hung in plain sight.

the firelight fell plainly upon a face, and owen had no difficulty in recognizing-- steve!

almost holding their breath the two boys watched to see what their strange chum did.

they saw him deliberately open the haversack and plunge his hand inside.

"oh! look! he's got the little package, max," whispered the horrified owen.

max pinched his arm.

"keep still," he made out to say in the other's ear.

he feared that owen's disturbed voice might have reached the ears of the prowler; but there was no sign to indicate such a thing.

indeed, steve went about his task with a deliberation that puzzled both the watchers.

"there! he's gone back to his blanket again," muttered owen, unable longer to keep still; "and max, did you see where he put that little packet which he believes holds all our prizes!"

"yes," replied the other, "inside that old extra coffee pot we fetched along to use in case anything happened to the one we have on the fire three times a day."

"that's the funniest thing i ever heard of, sure," continued owen. "he's crazy, that's what. who'd ever think of looking in that bum old coffee pot for anything worth while, tell me that, will you?"

"i can't. i'm all up in the air myself," admitted max.

"still, we saw him do it, didn't we! it wasn't a dope dream, was it, max!"

"i'm going to prove it pretty soon, owen."

"as how?" demanded the other.

"by getting that old coffee pot out here, and looking it over, that's how," replied the other.

"bully idea!" exclaimed owen, quickly. "say, looky here, perhaps now you really expect to find our other lost pearl in there?"

"wouldn't surprise me one little bit," chuckled max.

"oh! can't you sneak in now and crib the coffee pot?" begged owen.

"give him ten minutes to settle down," came the reply.

at the end of what seemed the longest ten minutes he had ever known, owen saw his agile cousin begin to move toward the opening of the tent.

on the way max picked up a long, stout stick that had a slight turn at the end. "he's going to fish for the coffee pot," whispered owen, in more or less delight; for he did so enjoy seeing max undertake anything that required brains.

the fishing met with speedy reward, for once the crook at the end of the pole had been inserted into the handle of the coffee pot, and the rest was easy.

so max came back to where he had left his comrade, bearing in his hands the old cooking utensil that thus far had not been needed, and might, if the other only held out, only prove a form of insurance against possible disaster.

deliberately max opened the coffee pot and thrust his hand inside.

"here's a package," he said, drawing something out.

"no need to open that," observed owen, quickly; "because we know it only holds the three poor pearls found in the catch brought in by the last squad. feel deeper, max. strike anything?"

for reply the other drew his hand out, nor did it come into view empty.

"the little cardboard box you put the first prize in," gasped owen. "please hurry and open it up, max."

his chum was no less eager to see what the contents of the box would prove to be.

no sooner had he removed the lid than the enraptured eyes of the two boys fell upon the lost pearl! yes, there it rested on its pink cotton bed, looking even more beautiful in owen's eyes than either of the two later prizes.

after staring at it for some time the boys allowed their eyes to exchange a look. max was pale and distressed, while his cousin, on the other hand, seemed to be excited, as though indignation and even anger had surged up within him.

CHAPTER XI.

the new cook springs his surprise.

"well, what d'ye think of that, eh?" owen exclaimed.

"it's hard to believe," replied the other.

"but all the same, we saw him with our own eyes, max," declared the other.

"yes, that's so," answered max, reluctantly.

"he took the first pearl; and meant to hide the other pair of beauties!" owen went on.

"looks like it," max admitted.

"then that ends it. steve dowdy can't train in our camp, or go along the same trail as we do, after this," and owen shook his head in a very determined way as he made this assertion.

"oh! hold your horses a little while, can't you, owen?"

"what! do you mean to give him another trial--is that it, max?"

"just one more, if we're lucky enough to find a prize," replied the other. "perhaps after all we'll have to use this jolly little milk-white chap over again."

"huh! i hope not," grumbled owen. "say, you mean to put it with the others in your pocketbook, don't you, and let the little box go empty?"

"of course. but try and forget all about this for a while, owen. give me another day to figure it out, please."

"say, i bet you've got an idea right now, max; you're always so quick to see through things."

"if i have i must think it over," replied the other.

"well, let me say this just once, and then i'll ring off for good," owen went on. "if he tries this same measly old game to-morrow night, you just ought to jump on steve, and demand to know what he means by treating his chums in this way."

max laughed a little.

"maybe i will, owen," he remarked. "the idea struck me before you mentioned it. just wait and see how things are going to turn out."

"but you'll bait the trap again, max, so steve'll know, or believe the game is worth the candle?"

"well, i guess yes," replied the other.

"how about telling toby or bandy-legs?" asked owen.

"better not," came the quick reply. "neither of them are worth shucks about keeping a secret, and chances are they'd give it away."

"just as you say, max. i depend on you to run this game down. but it makes me feel awful sore. i never would have believed it of good old steve."

"well, just hold your judgment in the air for a little while longer, owen," max said, calmly.

his cousin looked hard at him. then he shook his head as if completely puzzled.

"gee! but you do beat the dutch, max," he muttered. "i honestly reckon you're hoping to make me doubt what my own eyes saw. but, anyhow, i'm game to stand it out to the end."

"well, let's crawl in now with our blankets," suggested max.

"what! don't we keep watch any more, or wake up one of the others to take our place?" owen demanded.

"stop and think; what's the use?" chuckled max.

"glory! that's so. the performance is over for this night, anyhow. guess you're about right, max; and i do sure feel mighty sleepy."

so both boys managed to find the places reserved for them under the canvas, and slipped in without disturbing their comrades.

steve was rolled up in his blanket very much after the manner of a mummy. max cast a sharp look that way, and even bent over steve as he arranged himself in his rather cramped quarters.

"seems to be sleeping as sound as a bug in a rug," was his mental comment, as he caught the even and natural breathing of the suspected chum.

the balance of the night passed away without any further alarm.

when morning came toby and bandy-legs took max to task because he had not called on them to serve as sentinels over the camp.

"owen and i looked to that all right," max laughed back.

"then you are sure nobody made a sneak on us and got away with the second batch of prizes?"

it was bandy-legs who put this question. both toby and steve seemed intensely interested in the answer.

"sure, why, of course, we are," replied max, confidently. "nobody who didn't belong here had a chance to poke his nose into our tent last night."

toby and bandy-legs declared themselves satisfied with this assurance. as for steve, though he made no remark on the subject, his face seemed to indicate contentment.

"is it because he thinks he wasn't seen?" max kept asking himself, uneasily; but found no answer.

the plans for the morning were soon arranged.

steve was to pilot owen to the river over the trail he and max had made. and at the last moment toby begged for a chance to accompany the expedition.

"i w-w-want to show that i w-w-wasn't the jonah yesterday," he remarked, after max had said he could be spared.

"oh! rats!" spluttered bandy-legs, whose turn it was to attempt the cooking; but max thought he did not seem quite as cheerful as ordinarily.

max himself really meant to have a try in the marsh for woodcock, as they were known to frequent the low ground when feeding.

so the three boys went off, each with his empty bag, which he hoped to bring back partly filled with mussels, some of which might develop prizes when finally opened up.

bandy-legs pottered around the fire for a while, but max could see how unnaturally he acted.

"that boy's got something on his mind, it is dollars to doughnuts," he kept saying to himself, as he watched the nervous movements of the new cook.

this uncertainty caused him to postpone his departure in search of the only game available at that time of year. he thought he would hasten developments, and bring bandy-legs to the point.

"something bothering you a bit, old fellow?" he remarked, presently.

the other looked around uneasily.

"sure they won't come back on us yet a while, eh, max?" he asked, eagerly.

"no danger of that," assured max. "you can say what you want, and nobody will hear you."

"oh! max, it's dreadful," began bandy-legs.

"what is?" asked the other, though a sudden suspicion of the truth flashed through his mind.

"about steve. how could he be so mean?" bandy-legs went on.

"hello! what do you know about it?" demanded max.

"*i saw him!*" answered the cook, shaking his head in a dolorous fashion. "say, i've been thinking it over all the time. i was awake when you and owen came in. and somehow, max, i just feel awful about it. he must be half crazy to do such a thing."

"perhaps he is," admitted max, cautiously. "but look here, do you mean you were awake last night, and saw what steve did? is that it, bandy-legs?"

"yes. and, max, he put the pearls in our old coffee pot, would you believe it?" the other went on, excitedly.

max took out the stout little pocketbook which was intended for silver. as he opened this he remarked:

"hold your hand, bandy-legs."

"good gracious! two, three beautiful pearls! say, are they ours, the first one as well as the other two? and how did you get hold of them, max?" cried the other when he could catch his breath.

so, of course, max had to tell him the whole story.

"and we must keep mum about it till you play your hand; is that it?" asked the wondering and awestruck bandy-legs, at the conclusion of the recital.

"try and forget all about it, and act just the same as usual toward steve," said max.

the other agreed to do his best.

"but, max," he added, "i'm awful sore over it. steve dowdy was never known as having light fingers all the time i went to school with him. fact is, only that i saw him do it with my own eyes, nothing could make me believe steve a thief. oh! it's just rank!"

max sauntered off, gun in hand, while the cook busied himself about the fire. bandy-legs had brought his wonderful cookbook along. this contained dozens of recipes given him by the black "mammy" at home. these bandy-legs had written out after his own idea as to what should be used. but, perhaps, he may have misunderstood the directions in some cases; and the most astonishing results were apt to follow his attempt to surprise his campmates with some new dish calculated to tickle their healthy appetites.

he heard max fire frequently.

"run across game, all right," chuckled bandy-legs as he worked on industriously.

eating in all its phases appealed to bandy-legs; and the very thought of game for supper tickled his fancy.

when max did show up later on he was carrying a very nice little bundle of the long-billed woodcock with their attractive breasts.

"how many?" demanded bandy-legs, turning away from the fire where he had something boiling furiously.

"count and see," laughed max, placing his shotgun against a tree, and sitting down to rest.

"just five," remarked bandy-legs, presently; "say, that was mighty kind of you not to skip me, max. one apiece all around, eh? wow! i hope now my book tells just how woodcock are to be done, for blessed if i know a thing about it. to tell the honest truth, i don't recollect ever having seen the gamy-looking bird before."

"we'll manage that part of the programme all right, never fear, bandy-legs. pretty near time for the boys to be showing up, ain't it? hey! something's boiling over and trying to put out the fire."

with a whoop bandy-legs made a wild dash for his station, and apparently managed to "save his bacon," as max called out, laughingly.

presently the sound of voices told that the rest of the camping party had arrived.

each of them seemed to be carrying something of a load on his back.

the catch was heaped in a pile, and bandy-legs left his fire long enough to admire the product of the morning "wading act."

"get ready for dinner, you fellows," he remarked, with a trace of anxiety in his voice.

the rude table was set with the usual tin cups, pie pans for plates, knives, forks, and spoons. in addition there was a pile of bread, some cheese and crackers, part of a boiled ham, a mess of cold rice left over from the previous day, and a dish of hot boston baked beans.

"bring on the coffee," sang out steve, sitting down.

"s-s-say, what you got in the p-p-pot?" demanded toby, suspiciously.

"a surprise," grinned bandy-legs.

he filled four bowls with something from the pot and set them before his chums. it had a queer odor, and the boys sniffed at it first, looking toward each other.

toby was the first one bold enough to put a spoonful into his mouth.

"yum-yum!" he seemed to gurgle, and the others took this as an indication of approval, for immediately the three followed the example set by the "taster."

at once shouts and laughter went up, as every boy, even including the artful toby, made haste to get rid of his mouthful as fast as possible.

"ugh! what a horrible mess!" cried owen.

"what did you fool us for, toby?" demanded steve.

"huh! t-t-think i w-w-wanted all the t-t-taste to m-m-myself?" demanded toby.

"but whatever did you put in this stew to make it taste so funny?" demanded max.

"h-h-hope he didn't p-p-poison us?" broke out toby.

"why, i only put some salt in it," explained the cook, greatly broken up over his first attempt at "surprising" his chums.

"what did you take that salt out of?" asked owen.

"this little glass jar here; but what're you grinning at? ain't it salt at all?" demanded bandy-legs.

"taste it and see," owen fired back.

the cook did so, and made a wry face.

"baking soda!" he gasped; "and i spoiled my stew."

"and burnt it in the bargain," laughed max, remembering the boiling-over episode; "but there's plenty to eat besides. so pitch in, boys, and after we get through we'll see what sort of luck you had this morning."

CHAPTER XII.

danger ahead on the trail.

"look at steve!"

it was owen who muttered these three words in the ear of his cousin.

"yes, i've been keeping an eye on him," replied the other, uneasily.

it was to be expected that those who had gone off on the morning hunt for shellfish would show more or less eagerness to get at their catch, in order to learn just what sort of luck had attended their labors.

but long before either toby or owen had finished eating, steve hurried over to the pile, and squatting down, tailor fashion, began opening mussels.

just as the rest began to leave the vicinity of the fire they heard him give a shout.

"say, looky there at steve--he's dancing around like a wild injun!" cried bandy-legs.

"b-b-bet you he's f-f-found a jim-dandy p-p-pearl," spluttered toby.

all of them hastened over to where their comrade was carrying on so extravagantly.

"what you got, steve?" demanded bandy-legs.

"the best one yet, sure as you're born," and with these thrilling words steve opened his palm.

it was certainly a larger pearl than any they had yet found, and presented a more imposing appearance.

all of them crowded around to admire, and many were the pleased expressions which the young pearl hunters gave vent to.

"couldn't hardly believe my eyes when i saw that beauty lying in the shell," remarked the excited steve; "and the funniest part of it all is i picked up that shell myself."

"how d'ye know that?" asked owen. "there were two others along, perhaps you remember."

"sure," laughed steve, as pleased as a child, his eyes beaming, and his face flushed. "i'll tell you how it is, fellows. notice this queer mark like a five-pointed star on the shell? i remember stopping to look at it after washing the mud off the outside. gee! little did i suspect what i was holding in my hand."

"g-g-guess not," wabbled toby. "if you d-d-did i just reckon you'd g-g-gone ashore and b-b-b-b--"

of course, when toby floundered in the depths one of his chums as usual pounded him on the back vigorously; but that would not have wrought a cure only that the unfortunate stutterer managed to give his whistle, and then cry triumphantly:

"busted it open--there!"

"you just bet i would," admitted steve.

"say, we forgot to notice something," declared bandy-legs.

"as what?" asked owen.

"whether the shells of those other oysters that held prizes were also marked with a star," bandy-legs went on; at which the balance of the crowd laughed uproariously.

"what d'ye think of that?" cried steve. "he expects that when a mussel starts in to grow a nice healthy pearl he scratches a star on his shell to let the hard-working hunter know when he's struck a bonanza!"

"oh! my, how k-k-kind," chuckled toby.

"anyhow," asserted bandy-legs, stoutly, as he held the shell in question in his hand, "me to keep tabs when i'm doing the grabbing act this afternoon. and i give you all fair warning that if i do run across a shell with the star, i'm going ashore to open the same."

"good luck to you, then," laughed steve. "here, max, take charge of this, won't you, and put it with the rest of our prizes? i want to keep on opening shells, and see if my luck holds out."

max and owen exchanged a quick look.

apparently steve was perfectly sincere when he gave utterance to this natural remark. their bewilderment grew more and more, and both boys, as well as bandy-legs found it impossible to understand what it could mean.

max walked back to the tent as if meaning to deposit the pearl in the haversack along with the others. of course he would really slip it into his little leather coin purse where the three valuable pearls already reposed in safety.

"what d'ye make of him, max?"

owen asked this question as he bent over his chum, while the other was making a great pretense of handling the haversack.

"ask me something easy, please," the other replied, shaking his head from side to side.

"what bothers me is to understand why he called out, and let us all know he'd struck a find," owen continued.

"same here," max added.

"you'd think that if steve was the thief he seemed to be, his first act would have been to quietly pocket this big pearl, and just keep mum. ain't it so, max?"

"seems that way," came the ready answer. "to do that would save a heap of trouble in taking it out of the bag while the rest of us slept."

"but perhaps steve really enjoys that exciting part of the business," suggested owen.

"do you know, a thought struck me, though i can't take much stock in it," max went on.

"let's hear it, anyhow," remarked his chum.

"well, in order to make sure of the valuable pearls here, i'm putting them away in my private purse. well, what if some notion like that has struck our comrade, and he's hiding 'em unbeknown to us, either for a trick, or to make doubly sure they don't get lost."

owen sneered plainly, as if to express his disbelief in this far-fetched theory.

"it's just like you to try and screen a chum, old fellow," he observed; "but the idea seems too thin for me to take any stock in it. to tell the truth, i'd call it fishy. it won't wash, and you know it."

max sighed as he closed the bag that really held only the three next to worthless pearls.

"own up," persisted owen; "say that you just can't believe such a thing yourself, much as you'd like to."

"yes, it is so; there must be some other explanation that we haven't struck yet. but i believe i'm on the right trail. don't ask me any more, owen. to-night will see the answer, i reckon."

"hope so," grunted the other, and from his manner it was plain to be seen that owen did not share the sanguine spirit of his chum.

"now let's go back and see if there's anything doing with the rest of the fresh-water clams," suggested max.

but, although every shell was opened and carefully examined, only a couple of seed pearls were found, not worth mentioning alongside the four fine ones.

"anyhow," said toby, as the last mussel was passed, "it wasn't a s-s-skunk. we g-g-got one b-b-bully old p-p-prize, didn't we, steve?"

"me to look for the star brand of mussels!" declared bandy-legs; "they're the only kind worth toting to camp over that long trail."

it was max and bandy-legs who started out shortly after, bent upon new conquests.

"look out for him, max," said owen; "don't let him throw away all he finds, just because they don't happen to bear the star brand."

"oh! i'm not that big a silly," chuckled bandy-legs, starting off; "come on, max."

max saw a chance to remark in a low voice to his cousin:

"he knows all about it, and has promised to keep a close tongue."

"then you told him when you were alone here this morning?" remarked owen, and his tone announced that he doubted the propriety of confiding in bandy-legs.

"that's where you're away off," chuckled max. "fact is, he began to tell *me* about steve going to the bag in the middle of the night, and hiding something in the old coffee pot."

"you don't say?" exclaimed owen. "how the dickens would bandy-legs know about that?"

"happened to be awake and saw it all. so i thought i'd tell him what we knew, so as to make him keep a close mouth. i guess he won't leak, owen."

"then toby is really the only one out of the secret?" owen went on to say.

"yes. and there's no use telling him--yet. time enough to-night when we spring the trap. but i'm off now, after bandy-legs. so long, owen."

"be mighty careful about that coin purse," warned the one who was to stay in camp during the afternoon. "it would give me a big pain if you let it drop out of your pocket while you were wading in the river."

"can't. i've fastened the pocket up snug with a big safety pin," chuckled max.

he soon caught up with bandy-legs, who was following the now plainly marked trail that stretched through the forest between the river and the camp.

arriving at the water's edge max soon decided that it might pay them to work a little lower downstream.

so both removed most of their clothes and started to tread for the mussels that lay concealed in the mud or sand of the river's bed.

max was very careful to make sure that the little coin purse was safely pinned inside his shirt. he would not have risked leaving that ashore for a good deal.

an hour passed.

"i see you've picked up quite a little load," remarked max, as the two pearl hunters happened to come close together while continuing their work.

"all of two dozen, i reckon," grunted bandy-legs.

"many marked with the star brand?" asked max.

"shucks! never a single one, the more the pity," replied the other, grinning. "still, i live in hopes. found one that's got a cross on the shell. might be that's another mark to tell how the old hermit inside has taken to hatching out a pearl."

"well, let's make one more try of, say half an hour," proposed max.

"all right," agreed the other. "it's getting a little tiresome, i tell you. and i cut my toe on a sharp shell. sing out when the time's up, max. here goes to try along that point. looks promising there."

"yes, because some sort of a bar sets out from the shore. i'll head that way, too, only covering different ground."

max kept up the good work until the time limit had been reached. by then the two boys had about all the load they cared to carry over the trail to the camp.

"hope nobody holds us up on the way, and makes us hand over all we've got," suggested bandy-legs. "not that he'd get much out of me, because thirty-seven cents is about the limit of my fortune now; but i'm thinking of them pearls you carry, max."

"i've still left the coin purse pinned on the inside of my shirt," remarked max; "so the chances are he wouldn't be apt to find it on me."

they finished dressing, and, throwing the partly filled gunny sacks over their shoulders, started back along the trail for camp, max in the lead. "huh!" remarked bandy-legs, as he trotted along at the heels of his companion, "the fun about all this thing is the uncertainty of it. ain't that so, max?"

"it sure is," replied the other, without turning his head. "here we are, toting over five dozen mussels on our backs up and down, in and out, and we're just in a state of blissful eagerness and suspense. perhaps we carry a prize worth a whole vacation of sport; and then, again, chances are we draw a blooming blank."

"all right," remarked the cheerful max, "no matter how things turn out from now on, i don't see that any of us ought to kick. we've got four pearls that are bound to give us many times as much as we really hoped to earn. and that's enough to make us happy."

"it sure is, because now we'll be able to carry out all of those bully plans we made. wow! i c'n hardly believe it ain't all a dream, max," and bandy-legs drew a long sigh, as if trying to assure himself that he was really awake.

"you'll begin to believe it when we send off for our motorcycles, and map out the summer campaign," laughed max.

"glory be! that makes me thrill all over. if it does come to pass, won't we be the luckiest crowd that ever came down the pike?" assented bandy-legs.

"oh! i'd hardly say that," remarked the other. "we've worked for all we've got so far. the idea was, after all, the main thing, and we owe most of that to my cousin owen reading so much about how these pearls are found in indiana and missouri streams."

"oh! take care, max!" suddenly cried bandy-legs.

"what is it?" demanded the other, instantly.

"danger ahead; because i saw somebody poking a head out of the bushes there," bandy-legs went on, breathlessly.

CHAPTER XIII.

max plays the good samaritan.

max instantly dropped his sack of shellfish.

he had picked up a good stout stick, which he used as a cane while walking, poking ahead in every clump of bushes where it was possible a snake might lie coiled up in waiting.

bandy-legs had followed suit, and he, too, flourished a substantial hickory staff, which looked capable of doing good work in a pinch.

"now where did you see all this?" asked max.

"over yonder where that thick vine crawls all over things," came the quivering answer.

"all right; let's investigate then," suggested max, as he took a bold forward step.

at this demonstration bandy-legs gasped.

"say, are you really going to tackle him, max?"

"oh! i don't know," replied the other, carelessly, yet with a firm ring to his voice, and a determined look on his face. "if he's lying in wait to ambush us, we might as well turn the tables around, and start the ball rolling ourselves."

"but--gosh! he might have a gun!" suggested bandy-legs.

"let's hope not," max went on, cheerfully; "because that would be unfair, as we've left all our shooting-irons in camp. anyhow, it might pay us to put a bold face on the matter. so come along, bandy-legs."

"w-w-who's afraid?" gurgled the other, trying to look and act like his chum, though the effort was not wholly a success.

accordingly the two boys advanced straight toward the clump of bushes bordering on the camp trail, and which were overrun by the luxuriant vine.

"there he is again, max!" hissed bandy-legs.

"yes, i see him; and i reckon now that it's only that half-grown boy again, after all, bandy-legs."

the other gave a sigh, perhaps of relief.

"guess you hit the nail on the head that time, when you said what you did; because it's sure enough no big-bearded man waiting to hold us up. wonder what he wants with us, max?"

"don't you see he's beckoning right now?" asked the other, in a puzzled tone.

"that's right; but please go slow, max."

"why do you say that?" demanded the other, keeping his eyes on the eagerly beckoning boy who was emerging from the thicket.

"might be a trap, you know," bandy-legs went on. "heard about such things. the little critter may be just toling us on like they train a dog to do down in the duck regions along chesapeake bay."

"oh, rats!" max remarked. "that look of terror on his face ain't put on. you mark my words, bandy-legs, he's in a hole of some kind, and wants us to lend him a hand, see?"

"but where's the hole?" asked the other.

"oh! come off, won't you? i mean he's in trouble. but here we are, and we'll soon know."

as max said these last words he allowed a reassuring smile to creep over his face. he realized that the ragged boy was in some condition of genuine distress; and max had too kind a heart to even dream of adding to the poor lad's mental agony.

"hello! who are you, and what's the matter?" he asked, as they drew up alongside the smaller boy.

"i'm jim, mister, an' i'm in a heap o' trouble," the boy said, with an effort.

"well, jim, we want to be friends," max went on. "suppose you tell us what it's all about, won't you?"

something in his cheery tone, as well as the kind expression upon his face, seemed to give renewed confidence to the poor little chap.

this may have been the first time a stranger had ever spoken to him after such a fashion. perhaps he had had a cruel experience with the world, and was accustomed to looking upon all strangers as enemies.

but, now, the look of fear left his face, though there still remained that expression of agony.

"reckon as how he's goin' tuh cash in, stranger," he said; and max grasped the meaning of his words, although they were next door to greek to bandy-legs.

"who do you mean by saying he?" asked max.

"dad," answered the forlorn specimen, drawing down the corners of his mouth.

"is he sick?" continued max.

"nope. got hurted bad. falled down a big drop. reckon like he's a sure goner," the boy whimpered.

"where is he now?" the other asked, briskly.

"in our shack. he done crawled part way, an' wen i diskivered him i helped drag him home."

the lad said this latter a little proudly, as though he wanted these boys to understand that while he might look thin and puny, still he was not lacking in pure grit, and the ability to "do things."

"what do you want us to do, jim?" asked max.

"i seed yuh goin' along hyah, an' i thort as how p'r'aps yuh wont come over an' see dad. he's got a leg broke, that's flat; but yuh see he feels so pow'ful bad inside he's 'feared he's hurt thar. cain't yuh come 'long with me, mistah?"

not for a moment did warm-hearted max hesitate.

"sure we will. lead the way, jim. i suppose you can bring us back here again to get our bags of mussels," he said, promptly.

"i sartin kin, an' i will, mistah," replied the boy, a faint look as of hope appearing on his brown face.

"but, max--" whispered bandy-legs, plucking at his companion's coat sleeve.

"what ails you?" asked max, impatiently.

"is it safe, d'ye think?" demanded the other; "wouldn't it be better for us to go on to camp, pick up a gun, and then join jim here?"

"you can, if you want to." said max; "as for me, i'm going to believe in the story he tells."

but he did not throw away the stout stick which at the time he chanced to be carrying.

the boy had turned around. he wanted to see what they meant to do, and a new dread seemed to be gripping him.

but when max once again started forward, bandy-legs, as if a little ashamed of his suspicion, kept him company.

thus, following the uncouth little fellow closely, they began to pass through a very dense section of forest.

max considered that since they were going to all this trouble in order to do a good deed, it might be as well to learn a few things.

accordingly he quickened his pace, so that he drew up alongside jim.

"what's your dad's name, jim?" he asked.

the boy seemed to hesitate, as though even in his young mind he doubted the propriety of giving away family secrets.

"calls hisself tom jones, mistah," he finally replied; but max readily understood that the chances were the man had another name, which he did not like to own, as possibly it was connected with a prison sentence, or some crime.

however, max did not allow himself to feel any sort of curiosity in this direction. it was enough for him to know that the unfortunate man had fallen upon evil days, and was lying there with a broken leg, perhaps even dying, and far removed from all doctors.

"we've seen signs around that made us think you were collecting these mussel shells," he went on.

the boy nodded his head in the affirmative.

"no use denyin' it, mistah, 'case yuh'd see our shack wen yuh git thar, anyways," he muttered.

"and you've been thinking we'd come up here to beat you out in the game--is that it?" max continued.

another vigorous nod, and a gloomy look answered him.

"well, that's where you're away off, jim," max went on. "we don't care for the shells, and you're welcome to all we happen to gather, after we've taken out and eaten the meat. i suppose your dad means to get a load down the river, and sell the same to some factory that manufactures pearl buttons?"

"yep. an' we was a gettin' heaps o' 'em; but if dad he draps off, it's all busted," jim replied.

his manner told max that at least he must cherish a certain amount of affection for his father.

"ain't we nearly there?" grunted bandy-legs, who had proven clumsy, so that several times, catching a foot in some concealed creeper, he had almost fallen flat.

"jest a leetle bit furder, mistah," replied jim, eagerly, as though he feared that these new-found friends might grow suspicious or weary, and desert him in his time of great need.

five minutes later and they stepped into a little open space. the hill rose abruptly before them. max realized that they must be close to the camp of the shell gatherers, even before he saw this opening, for he could detect an odor in the air far from delightful, and which he knew must come from a collection of hundreds and hundreds of shells, many of them possibly recently opened.

jim's father had found a natural cave under a great shelf of rock that jutted out from the base of the hill.

here the two were safe from the violent summer storms; and with a couple of worn blankets, a few cooking utensils, and a scant allowance of food, they were able to carry on the business of gathering the fine shells, with their mother-of-pearl lining, so necessary in the button trade.

several piles of shells caught the eyes of the two boys as they approached the strange camp.

max, however, looking farther, discovered a form upon the ground, partly covered by a blanket.

a dreadful suspicion came over him that the man might have died while jim was seeking help. this, however, was speedily dissipated, for he saw "tom jones" raise himself on one arm and stare hard at them.

fear was in those burning dark eyes, such fear as might be shown by a fugitive from justice, one who believed every honest man's hand was raised against him.

but max would not allow himself to even think of this. the poor fellow was in trouble; he needed help the worst kind, and it was no business of theirs to ask questions.

"we've come to see if we can help you, mr. jones," he remarked, in his customary cheery tone, as he bent over the injured man.

"jim got yuh, did he?" muttered the other. "knowed 'twar the on'y thing tuh be did, no matter wat follered."

"make your mind easy, because there's nothing going to follow. now, it happens that even if i am only a boy, i've always had an itching to be a surgeon some day. so i know a little about setting broken bones. i'm going to play doctor, if you'll let me, mr. jones."

as max said this he stripped off his coat. the boy watched him in awe, while the man showed signs of newly awakened hope.

for quite some time max examined his patient, even turning the man over so that he could test his ribs thoroughly.

"now i'm going to set that leg the best i can, with splints to hold it. after all it's a simple fracture a little way above the ankle. those black and blue marks don't count for anything, mr. jones. make up your mind you're going to pull through nicely. you were lucky, for it might have been much worse."

"but i'm sore up in the body," said the man.

"yes, you're bruised some, and i expect a rib or two may be broken. but they'll mend all right. don't worry for a minute. i'll come and see you again once or twice before we go back to town. and i'm going to send you up some things from the store."

the man could hardly express his gratitude, but max saw tears in his eyes. he was ragged and wore a rough beard, but his face was not unkind. and jim seemed to set considerable store by his father, which would indicate that the boy was not abused.

"gettin' shells, too, i reckon?" the man remarked, as max shook hands with him preparatory to leaving.

"well, no," replied max, and then, obeying a sudden inspiration, he went on; "it might pay you after this to carefully examine the *inside* of every fresh-water clam you gather, because we've found some good pearls that are worth ten times as much as all your shells. good-by, tom jones. i'm coming again to-morrow to see you, and bring some coffee and bacon. now, jim, show us the way back to where we left our sacks."

CHAPTER XIV.

setting the man trap again.

jim was only too delighted to act once more as guide.

the look of fear had quite left his face, and both max and bandy-legs saw that after all the poor little chap was rather a decent-looking boy.

"say, is he agoin' tuh git well, mistah?" he asked, turning when they were once more fairly on the way back to the trail leading to the camp.

"sure he is, jim," answered max.

"but he'd 'a' gone dead on'y for you uns comin' tuh help. reckon as how we orter be kinder 'bleeged fur doin' this away," went on the boy, awkwardly trying to prove that he knew what gratitude meant.

"that's all right, jim," max smilingly said. "perhaps he wouldn't have died on account of his broken leg, but he'd never walked again without a limp. but look here, don't you say another word about it, jim."

"but--"

"because," max went on, quickly, "it's been a pleasure to me to attend your dad. i'm wanting to be a surgeon some day, and every little bit of practice helps. now, if you don't mind, we'd like to know something about you, jim. where'd you come from? i never saw you or your father around carson, which is the name of the town where my chum here and myself live."

the boy actually turned red in the face. his confusion told the sharp-eyed max that there must be some sort of unpleasant story connected with the past.

"hold on, jim, i take that back," he hastened to say. "it's none of my business, and you needn't tell me anything about what you've been through."

"but i jest has tuh, 'case it's been a-burnin' in here ever so long, an' never anybody tuh tell," and jim slapped his hand on his breast as he spoke.

"oh! well, please yourself, jim," max observed, seeing that the confidence would really satisfy the boy, who had evidently never known a friend in all his life, save his wandering father.

"and, jim," put in bandy-legs, seriously, "just you make up your mind that we'll never whisper a word of what you tell us to a living soul, eh, max?"

"that's a sure thing," replied the other.

jim fell back a little, so that he might be closer to these two splendid friends, who were already assuming the rï¿½le of heroes in his eyes.

"'tain't so bad, i reckons," he started in to say. "yuh see, dad, he never done as they sez. lots o' times he tells me as how sum other man he tries tuh rob that ole farmer. but they ketched him in our camp, an' totes him tuh the farmhouse. i heerd 'em say as how they means tuh kerry dad tuh town an' hev him shut up, when mawnin' kims along."

the boy drew a long breath. his eyes flashed with the memory of the wrongs that had been heaped upon his father; and max chuckled with glee to see that after all he had more or less "spunk" in his small body.

"i take it from what you say, jim, that you weren't made a prisoner at the same time they nabbed your father?" he remarked.

"naw," replied the boy, "i chanct tuh be away from camp jest then, yuh see. wen i kim back i seed three big men a-hustlin' dad along, an' him a-saying all' ther time he never done nawthin'."

"of course you followed them?" said max.

"yep. they wasn't nawthin' else tuh be done," came the answer, as the boy grinned a little.

"bet you he helped his dad skip out, max," was the suggestion bandy-legs put up.

"did you, jim?" demanded the other.

"i sartin did that same, mistah," came the prompt reply, a little proudly. "seen whar they done locked dad in the smokehouse. tried the door, but it wa'n't no go. then i started tuh tunnel under the wall."

"well, i declare! what d'ye think of that, now?" exclaimed the wondering bandy-legs. "ain't he just the little boss schemer, though?"

"and did you succeed--did you get your dad out all right?" asked max.

"i sartin did. took a heap o' time, i tell yuh. reckon 'twas nigh mawnin' wen he crawled through the hole, an' we lit out foh the woods."

"and since that time you've been in hiding, afraid to show yourselves in any town?" max continued, bent on knowing all the particulars, for he had taken a decided interest in little jim.

"yep, we jest stuck tuh the woods," the other went on to say. "dad, he 'membered hearin' some feller say as how these yer shells was wuth money, if so be they cud be gathered in heaps. an' so yuh see we ben gatherin' 'em right along."

"how'd you ever get feed?" asked bandy-legs, whose mind always traveled to this very important question.

"dad had jest a leetle money, left over from his last job," jim replied. "then we set traps an' ketched a few rabbits. i fished some, too. reckon we managed tuh get along. lots o' times, though, i was that hungry i cud 'a' et a raw turnip."

"you say your father worked--was he a farm hand?" max asked.

"naw. dad he's a travelin' printer, an' a good un, too, mistah. but he jest cain't stay ennywhere long. he's got gypsy blood, yuh see, and the travel bug he sez is in his body. so arter a little we gets out on the road again tuh see the sights."

"a traveling printer, eh?" remarked bandy-legs; "say, that's kind of queer now. reckon he'd strike a job if he dropped in on mr. robbins, the editor of the *carson weekly town topics*."

"what makes you say that?" demanded max.

"because i chanced to hear him say his typesetter was bound to leave him in the lurch, and he didn't know where he'd get a man by the first of the month," bandy-legs replied promptly.

"there, do you hear that, jim?" remarked max.

"yep. but reckons as how it ain't a-goin' tuh do we uns any good," answered the boy, dejectedly.

"why not? by that time your dad's leg ought to be fairly well. and a couple of us boys could take him down to carson soon in one of our boats."

jim looked into the face of his kind friend while max was speaking. there were tears in the little chap's eyes.

"reckon yuh done forget, mistah!" he sighed.

"now you mean about the trouble your dad fell into on account of that old farmer; is that it, jim?" demanded max.

the boy nodded his head in a forlorn fashion.

"how long ago was this, jim--about a month?" max asked.

"reckon she be all o' that, mistah."

"and did you hear the name of the old farmer whose house had been robbed, jim?"

"i never done forgot that. i seems tuh heah it whispered by every leetle wind thet blows. wenever i waked up in the night it kim a-stealin' along past the ledge o' rock, an' makin' me shiver. i tell yuh. he was a orful hard-lookin' ole man, mistah."

"but perhaps not quite so hard as he seemed, jim. was that name griffin, jim?" asked max.

"yep," piped the boy, shivering; "an heah's them two bag o' mussels, jest whar yuh left 'em."

"all right, jim. i didn't expect they'd be stolen. now listen to what i say, jim."

"yas, suh."

"when you go back to your dad tell him i said he needn't be afraid to show himself in carson, or any other town around these diggings; because the tramp who robbed old griffin's place was caught, and all the stuff found on him!"

"that's right," interrupted bandy-legs, anxious to have a part in the developments; "and i saw the chief of police bring him into town, too. he was sure a tough-looking case. your dad looks like a gentleman beside that hobo thief."

"old griffin is a just man," max went on. "i'm sure he's felt sorry for treating your father as roughly as he did, without having any evidence against him. and if you two showed up at his place to-day chances are he'd take you both in and give you jobs."

"but," said bandy-legs, "there ain't no need of that. i'm bent on seeing tom jones get that vacancy on the local paper."

"is tom jones your father's real name?" asked max. "you needn't be afraid to say, jim, because nobody is going to harm him now."

"it's thomas archer. he kin talk jest as good as you kin, wen he wants tuh to do it. but the fellers we tramps with done lawf at him, so he larns tuh talk like they does. but yuh done makes me happy, tell yuh, mistah. glad now i waited on the trail foh yuh."

"you belong down south, don't you, jim?" asked max.

"reckon nawth car'liny was the place i was borned into this world, suh, but i don't jest see how yuh guessed that," the boy answered.

"never mind. suppose you trot along with us to our camp now. i'd like to send back a few things, like coffee and bacon, for your dad and you."

jim could only clutch the hand of max when he said this and squeeze it. but the other felt something moist drop on the back of his hand, and was sure it must be a tear.

the boys were once more taken in charge, and their interrupted march along the trail resumed.

when they entered the camp various were the exclamations of surprise from the three who had been left in charge.

of course a perfect rain of questions followed, and for some time both max and his fellow laborers in the shellfish industry were kept busily employed answering these interrogations.

finally, as the sun was sinking low, jim was allowed to depart, fairly laden with the various good things which the campers insisted on sending to the unfortunate tramp printer.

"we can spare them easy enough," max had remarked.

"sure we can, and more, too," echoed owen.

"b-b-besides, we've b-b-been so lucky, you k-k-know, in our hunt for p-p-pearls, we ought to be g-g-g-g--"

again came the usual pounding on the back, which produced no results; but as soon as toby could pucker up his lips, so as to whistle, he immediately calmed down enough to shout at the top of his voice:

"generous--there!"

"well, i should say we could," observed steve, rubbing his hands together exultantly. "even if we did lose that first beaut of a gem, haven't we still got three elegant ones? and perhaps you fellows may have fetched the mate of the lost one along in this last batch. you never can tell."

max could not help looking toward owen, who raised his eyebrows after a peculiar fashion that could only stand for bewilderment.

steve certainly had these three loyal chums guessing. but max was fully determined that the mystery must not remain such over another night, if he could arrange matters so that the solution might be hastened.

to this end he presently started to assist bandy-legs open their catch of the afternoon, steve and toby being engaged in getting supper.

another prize rewarded their search, a pearl not so fine as the one steve had discovered, but so perfect in shape, and so milk-white in color, that they agreed it ranked with any of the rest in value.

so max was very careful to wrap this last prize up in some paper, and thrust it into the haversack, with all his comrades looking on, especially steve. the latter stared as usual, as though fascinated by the sight of the beautiful gem.

"he'll try again, my word on it," whispered bandy-legs in the ear of max; whereupon the other put a finger on his lips to enjoin silence.

the five boys spent the evening as usual in merry conversation and song. all seemed to be in high spirits, even steve joining with a vim in the school songs so dear to their hearts.

then, as the hour grew later, they began to yawn; and first toby crawled inside the tent, then owen, and finally steve, bandy-legs, and max.

apparently the idea of keeping guard over the camp had been abandoned, now that they knew jim and his father were honest.

a long time passed, with only the heavy breathing of the boys to disturb the silence. the fire, prepared by max ere he turned in, continued to burn briskly.

it must have been midnight again when owen felt the hand of his cousin shake him, and, raising his head a little, he saw that there was something doing.

CHAPTER XV.

the mystery solved--conclusion.

steve was on his hands and knees, and apparently in the act of getting to his feet.

strangely enough he did not seem to show any sign of nervousness or caution; and owen looked in vain to see the suspected thief glance suspiciously around, as though to observe whether his comrades were all sound asleep at the time.

bandy-legs did not stir, and, judging from his heavy regular breathing, he must have dropped asleep, despite his intention of staying awake.

the exertions and excitement attending that afternoon tramp had proven too much for bandy-legs, and neither of the others thought it worth while to awaken him.

truth to tell, both max and owen were staring at steve, holding their very breath with surprise.

the other had by now reached the pole of the tent to which the strap of the haversack was attached. they could plainly hear him grumbling to himself as he thrust his hand inside.

drawing out the little wad of paper in the midst of which max had secured the latest find, steve could be seen carefully closing the bag again.

he did not look around once to see if he was observed, a fact that puzzled owen greatly; but passing over to where the cooking outfit lay he calmly picked up the extra coffee pot, raised the lid, pushed the packet in with the other stuff that seemed to lie hidden there, and once more placing the strange pearl bank down, steve made his way back to his blanket.

he stepped over the forms of toby and bandy-legs while so doing, and never once touched them with his feet. max believed he could hardly have duplicated the act, and his astonishment increased accordingly.

steve seemed to give a satisfied grunt as he settled down again under his blanket. it was about what one would emit after having felt that he had done his duty.

owen heard max laughing softly to himself.

"what does it all mean, max?" he whispered, as he heard steve begin to breathe regularly once more.

"tell you in the morning," replied the other. "too long a story for now. besides, i want steve to be around at the time, you see."

"that's mean of you," grumbled the disappointed one.

"can't help it; go to sleep and don't worry, owen."

"but, say, hadn't we better make sure of that last pearl? it goes against my grain to have such valuables kicking around in old coffee pots," owen protested.

"shucks! then you didn't see me palm the pearl. i put a pebble in place of it. right now that pearl is in my coin purse, keeping company with the rest," and max chuckled again as he snuggled down under his blanket.

"gee! you're a wizard, all right," said owen, in a whisper, as he reluctantly followed suit.

no doubt he lay awake for a long time, puzzling his head for a solution of the mystery. but the balance of the night passed, and morning found the boys wide awake, hungry, and ready for another day at the delightful task they had set for themselves.

it was when breakfast was about over that max chose to spring his little surprise.

steve had just announced his intention of being in the party that would follow the trail to the river that morning.

"hope i duplicate my luck of yesterday, fellows," he was saying, with a big sigh, when max, leaning forward so as to catch his eye, remarked:

"by the way, steve, do you happen to remember having any odd little tricks as a kid--anything that'd be apt to give your mother and father cause for anxiety *in the night?*"

bandy-legs, who had been secretly told concerning the happenings of the night, held his breath; owen, too, immediately assumed an eager look, and toby, not knowing what it was all about, stopped eating, and listened.

"in the night--we have tricks, you say? now, whatever in the wide world can you mean?" asked the apparently astonished steve.

"well, like walking in your sleep let's say," continued max. "did you ever do such a thing, steve?"

the other grinned and looked a little foolish.

"i sure did, when i was a kid, and it's a fact, fellows," he admitted. "but, say, i've been cured of that a long time."

"you *think* you have, you mean?" max persisted, while owen and bandy-legs exchanged a look of intense relief, now beginning to grasp the theory that max was working along.

"haven't done any stunts that way for nearly five years, give you my word, boys!" declared steve, looking a little worried at the same time.

"oh! yes, you have, steve," laughed max. "you've fallen back into your old bad ways again, it seems. for the last few nights you've been prowling around our camp here, and giving me the biggest shock ever."

"you don't say?" exclaimed the other. "what did i do, max. tell me right away, please."

"well, you seemed to have our precious pearls on your mind all the while."

"good gracious! i hope now i didn't try--say? did i go anywhere near that old haversack?" demanded steve, plainly embarrassed.

"every time, straight for it," replied max.

"and took something out?" pursued steve.

"your one object," said max, "seemed to be a terrible fear that some thief might rob us. and so as to block this little game you set out to hide the pearls in a new place."

"as where?" demanded the astounded steve.

"remember the second coffee pot we fetched along? well, you hit on that as the new hiding place"; and even as max spoke, the other, scrambling to his feet, hastened over to where the spare cooking utensils lay. coming back with the extra coffee pot he proceeded to drag out its contents.

when the papers and the little cardboard box that contained pink cotton had all been opened, with the result that only the pebble and the few less valuable pearls were found, steve stared in dismay.

"oh! they're all gone!" he cried, hoarsely. "i've lost the whole bunch, just because i kept thinking about them so much, and worrying about their being stolen. whatever will we do, max?"

"we don't have to do anything," replied the other, with a laugh, as he drew out his coin purse; "because i've got every one of the little beauties safe right here."

"even the one that was lost first of all," spoke up bandy-legs, as though proud to show that he had been in the secret right along.

steve's hand trembled when max emptied the little white objects into his palm. and perhaps there were tears in his eyes, even as there was certainly a suspicious quiver to his voice as he went on to say:

"that's a low-down trick of mine, boys, and this time it came mighty near blocking all our fine plans by losing the pearls that are going to get us the money we need. don't ever leave anything valuable lying around while i'm in camp. it works on my mind, i guess. ugh! ain't i glad you saw me do it? how tough we'd feel if none of us could give a guess where the blessed little things had gone. here, put 'em away again, max. it sure ain't safe for a feller with my failing to be handling such pretty things."

max, of course, did put them away securely. but his heart as well as those of owen and bandy-legs felt much lighter.

now that suspicion had given way to a knowledge of steve's sleep-walking weakness, they could look out in the future, and guard against such a thing.

and all of them were happy in the conviction that their comrade's fair name had been entirely cleared, for steve would have been sorely missed had he been dropped from the list of members in the club.

although those who went out returned with a fair bag, no reward followed the opening of the bivalves.

"p'r'aps we've cleaned up the old river, and there ain't another pearl to be found," suggested bandy-legs.

the others were loth to accept this view of the case; and for several days they searched industriously for the now elusive fresh-water clams.

"guess we'll have to call it off," remarked max, when on the third day the hunters came back with a scant dozen mussels, none of which yielded a profitable harvest.

"but seems to me we've got all we need, and several times over," owen declared, positively.

"all in favor of returning to carson to-morrow hold up a hand," suggested max.

he saw four hands instantly raised.

"that makes it unanimous," he laughed; "and i guess i can see what ails you all. it's how much are we going to get for our catch; and will the money buy the five motorcycles we're aiming to get."

"likewise supply us with a fund to purchase grub while on our trip," remarked bandy-legs.

"hear! hear!" sang out toby, who always agreed with his rival whenever the question of eating arose.

"i've an idea we don't need to worry about that," declared owen, confidently.

"what about jim and his daddy?" asked steve.

"we'll have to make a stretcher, and carry the man down to our boats," replied max.

"his leg is knitting bang-up," asserted owen, as he cast a proud look toward his cousin and chum.

"well, let's get busy here, so we can leave early in the morning," max remarked, hastily, for he was modest, and did not like praise.

they set to work with a vim, and the packing was speedily accomplished.

then in the morning all the stuff connected with the camp was carried down to the river and carefully loaded in the two boats, which, of course, were found safely just where they had been left.

after that, tom archer was carried on a rude litter, and made comfortable in one of the boats.

it was about the middle of the afternoon when the little expedition reached carson.

one of the ted shafter gang saw them come in and managed to get word to his leader, as well as shack beggs. the three gaped to see a lame man carried to a wagon, and asked many questions; but had to restrain their curiosity until the story became known through the community.

when it was learned that the mussels along the big sunflower had yielded up a number of fine pearls, said to be quite valuable, everybody in town, and not a few eager men in the bargain, set to work searching the adjacent waters.

but, apparently, max and his chums must have about exhausted the mine of good luck, for when every mussel within twenty miles of carson had been caught, the result was so meagre that the searchers gave up the new "get-rich-quick" game in disgust.

true to their promise the boys saw the editor of the weekly paper, and just as soon as he was able to limp, with the aid of a crutch, to the print shop, tom archer began work at the case.

he vowed he would try and curb his roving spirit so that little jim might have a chance to get some schooling in the fall.

and both jim and his father declared they owed more than words could express to max, who had brought light when the darkness was greatest.

what about the pearls?

well, two of them were taken into the city and pronounced as fine as any discovered through the famous fresh-water pearl industries located along the rivers of indiana and other states.

when max told the amount that was deposited in bank to their credit, his four chums were fairly wild with delight.

"let's send off right away for our motorcycles and get started on our trip!" cried steve, impatiently.

"and be sure to get mine with a short tread, because, you know, i haven't got the reach the rest have," observed bandy-legs, cautiously.

in due time the five motorcycles were ordered, and then a period of anxious waiting followed.

what wonderful plans these five chums had in view when the machines finally arrived, and had been fairly mastered, will be given in detail in the pages of the next volume of this series to be entitled: "the rivals of the trail."

the end.

Breinigsville, PA USA
22 June 2010

240411BV00004B/77/P